Under the Influence

Creator Love

Ankush Bahuguna @ankushbahuguna

One of my first memories of MissMalini is meeting her at an event and just clinging onto her, not letting her go because I was new to Mumbai and very awkward. I didn't know how to approach people or say hi to them. MissMalini is so warm, and she just brings people together. That's what I love about her.

Anushka Mitra @anushkamitra

I started reading the blog MissMalini in 2008 to stay up-to-date with all the gossip and entertainment in Bollywood because it was a reliable source. MissMalini's content is authentic; she curates content that keeps her audience hooked. Malini has impacted my career through her communication skills. She communicates very smoothly. I've also seen her anchoring and hosting, which is what I do. So I've picked up some traits from her. All of this is extremely inspiring, so thank you.

Avanti Nagral @avantinagral

I stumbled upon MissMalini before I even entered the creator industry, and I was so in awe of this boss woman who had built a whole industry from scratch. Malini has constantly reinvented herself. She's evolved from being an RJ, a dancer, a businesswoman to a creator. Of course, MissMalini is a phenomenal success story but Malini the human is so much more, and it's such a joy and pleasure to be able to call her a friend, an inspiration and a mentor.

Dimpi Sanghvi @dimpisanghvi_ws

The earliest memory I have of meeting Malini was at an awards event in Abu Dhabi. She was interviewing the celebrities on the red carpet, as was I. In fact, I interviewed her as well for the brand I was representing at the event and she was so much fun, confident and down to earth. I instantly took a liking to her and since then she is someone who inspires me a lot. I call her a superwoman because of the zillion things she does and excels at. Malini is so full of life and I wish she keeps soaring to new heights each day.

Dolly Singh @dollysingh

My first memory of MissMalini is when I went to Fashion Week as this little kid who had a fashion blog. Malini she was there, strutting around meeting everyone, giving everyone flying kisses. I looked from a distance and thought, Oh my God. Like, look at her. Like, look at her! And now she's here today, interviewing and meeting us, and it's just amazing how far she has come … It's amazing that she sustained this for fifteen years. It's her feat, and I congratulate the whole team that has also made it happen.

Elton Fernandez @eltonjfernandez

I first met Malini in the office which was located near Rajesh Khanna garden. She was wearing a little white dress and a flower in her hair, and I remember thinking, I don't know what I'm doing here. I had never done a shoot in a little office space or done makeup by an open window with the sunlight beaming through. Malini then said to me that I should do something on YouTube, which I went on to do. A couple of years later, I was on a YouTube fan fest selling tickets alongside Superwoman. So that was a milestone for me. Malini is a visionary; she has a unique knack of spotting talent and success in young people and being able to direct them towards that.

Karishma Govil @soul_kari

I've been very fortunate to have had really good women role models and mentors to inspire me. They include my grandmother, my mom, my sister. And one of the most important women is Malini, because she is my work mom with whom I started my writing and content creation journey. Before Malini, I was a salesperson and she is solely responsible for the shift in my life. I've learned so much from her because she's a great mentor. She is also what she preaches. She is a bundle of positivity. You can rely on her 24/7, and I love that about her.

Kusha Kapila @kushakapila

Congratulations to MissMalini on completing fifteen years. You are such an OG, the one who started it all, the one who knew 'influence' before influencers were a thing. I remember going on to the website and checking what's happening because, you know, she had the tea before tea was even a thing. So congratulations, MissMalini! I hope you continue to thrive and continue to give us the best in entertainment.

Malvika Sitlani @malvikasitlaniofficial

I grew up watching MissMalini and she was everything for me. She was exactly who I wanted to be. So thank you for giving us the ultimate platform to be inspired by because that gave us content creators the confidence to do what we do despite all our insecurities. MissMalini is a legacy!

Nirmika Singh @nirmika

I was studying journalism in Delhi and one of my dissertations was about the changing face of media. Content was rapidly evolving, moving away from print to digital. It was a moment of confusion. That was also when I first came across MissMalini and her refreshing brand which was a great mix of curation, journalism and blogging. She had mixed many different worlds to give people a whole new universe of content. She was a visionary. MissMalini is a pioneer of the Indian creator economy, and nobody can ever take that crown away from her. She wears that crown with a lot of grace. Every time I've been in a room with Mal, I've felt more visible because she uplifts people. She literally has your back and gives you wings that you didn't even know that you had.

Parul Kakad @mumbaimummy

I know I say this all the time, but I've seen you grow from Malini to MissMalini. I met you nineteen years ago, during which I've witnessed fifteen years of you building this company from sitting solo on your couch to creating this gigantic network and system. I still remember our excitement over twenty daily hits on the blog, not even realizing that you'd one day reach over 600 million across various platforms.

Sir Shah Rukh Khan once said, 'I will keep working until everyone has my name on their lips.' And I see you're doing this with the same motivation and drive you hold within your mind, body, and soul. You've not only inspired me but also millions of others, proving you can come to Mumbai with just one suitcase and make dreams come true. You're an inspiration to not just young people, but to individuals across any field and age.

You're a powerhouse boss lady who pulls people together to create businesses, career opportunities and so much more. But the most important thing is, you do it with love, kindness and empathy. I'm going to ask you this on behalf of most people who know you: How do you do it? The moment you open your eyes, you're like a light bulb that just turns on, and you're on the run. But the best part is that not only do you turn on your bulb, you also switch on an entire circuit that motivates people for the day! You've always said one thing that's stuck with me: Never say or write anything about anyone that you can't say to their face! That's a trait everyone should embody, individually or as a company. You've maintained that spirit and set an example in both aspects of your life. And I love that about you. Not only are you a legend on your own, you've also created an era! The MissMalini Era!

Pooja Dhingra @poojadhingra

I remember passionately reading MissMalini when it was a blog. Her blog was our way of knowing what was going on in Bollywood. This also gives you a clue about my age! But what I love and admire is that both the person and the platform have evolved and moved with the times, and so she is always relevant, constantly learning and tackling challenges. Malini is super inspiring.

Prabhat @Iamprabhatchaudhray

I met Malini a few years ago at a BMW rally in Nasik. Till then, I had only heard of Malini and had known of her as the biggest celebrity in the influencer world. I, on the other hand, had just come to Mumbai a couple of years earlier, and had thought to myself 'don't think Malini will even speak to a small-town introvert like you'. But not only did she speak to me, Malini also made me feel extremely comfortable, and she invited me to be a part of the group. She's one of the most non-judgmental, perceptive and inclusive people ever, who only sees the positives in everyone. What I love about her is that she believes in the collective growth of the community and goes the extra mile to help other creators grow and flourish. I have learnt so much from her and she has always had my back! For someone like me who came to a new city, a new industry with no backing or friends, Malini Agarwal has been one of my pillars of strength and support and I shall value and cherish her presence in my life forever.

Prajakta Koli @mostlysane

My first memory of MissMalini is when I was a radio intern and I was tasked with interviewing Deepika Padukone for *Finding Fanny* (2014); I was also told to do a good job because MissMalini was going to be there and she would also be conducting an interview. I remember Googling MissMalini. Nitish, who was an intern with me at the time, told me, 'Bro, MissMalini is like everything Bollywood; she is the real deal,' and I was like, 'I can't wait to meet her here,' though I never did, and I remember thinking, Ooh, who is this MissMalini? But now look at us!

Ranveer Allahbadia @beerbiceps

My first impression of MissMalini was when I was in engineering college, when I found out that there was a digital social media internet entrepreneur who was growing a business through blogging. It was extremely aspirational for me, straight out of college. When my own career started in 2015, I studied MissMalini to understand how to monetize an internet business in the first place. That's what I think most people have learned from her—that she has an extremely sharp business mind, which is the only way it should be.

Reshma Bombaywala-Lezinska @reshmabl

My friendship with Malini goes back to the time when she was still writing for *Midday*. We have seen each other through many different phases of our lives. She has stayed consistent and true to her personality, essentially being this really effervescent, positive, happy, kind, helpful person who's always quick to laugh. I am truly privileged and honoured that I can call her my friend.

Rij Eappen @kingofclubsin

I first met Malini almost two decades ago when she was a radio jockey. What struck me as remarkable was that she was a consummate people person who brought people together and found immense joy in connecting them. It didn't come as much of a surprise that what she did with MissMalini paved the way for the entire Indian blogging industry, and that's why she's hailed as India's first influencer, inspiring a generation of people to follow in her footsteps. Her dream of bringing the entire Indian creator ecosystem together with her ventures is awe-inspiring.

Rizwan Bachav @rizwanbachav

MissMalini was blogging before the word 'blogger' existed. So, for me, she's the OG when it comes to blogging, entertainment and lifestyle. During 2009–10, everyone went to MissMalini to check out what was happening, the latest in the entertainment and lifestyle space. So even before I knew Malini personally, I knew about her blog. That was my introduction to her. And, of course, through my social circle when I met her. She's a fabulous person. What she's done in this space has been a phenomenal fifteen years now, and I'm sure there's fifty more to go. All the best, Malini, and keep entertaining all of us.

Rohan Shrestha @rohanshrestha

In 2008, the way MissMalini blew up was interesting because there was nothing like it back then when there was no social media. Then I got a chance to work with her and it's been such a pleasure. Malini has helped boost my career growth. She's always been there when I've needed help. And that's a testament to her character and personality. Congratulations on your second book! It's fantastic.

Shashank Sanghvi @iamshashh

My earliest memory of meeting Malini was at an event in Bandra. I always knew that she was the famous MissMalini and I was very fascinated when I met her. She was so warm and welcoming. Malini is a superwoman. I always tell her whenever I meet her. She is everywhere and full of energy, doing so many things in the world of glitz and glamour! Malini is an inspiration to so many people! She is so much fun and full of life whenever we meet! I am so glad to have met her and know her personally. Wishing you all the love, good health, happiness and more success.

Shibani Bedi @shibani_bedi

Congratulations, MissMalini for completing fifteen years! You're a maverick of the entertainment industry, covering events, entertainers, fashion in the most unique way possible. You had a voice of your own, which set you apart from websites and journalistic portals that were doing that kind of reporting. And

I hope there is more. Here's to many more years of glory and amazing content!

Shivani Bafna @shivani_bafna

I was eighteen when I first met Malini. All my life I wanted to become a doctor and study biomedical engineering. But I'd followed MissMalini for many, many months and love Bollywood. One day, I saw a post that MissMalini was looking for interns. So, I was like, you know what, let me just try. I got to Mumbai. And when I say that Malini is single-handedly the reason that I'm not a doctor today, it's not an understatement. I think she exposed me to the fact that there's a world that's beyond conventional careers and it's possible to make a living off of doing something that you're passionate about. I didn't know that world even existed if it weren't for the opportunity to intern at MissMalini. So just giving me that confidence and exposure, and showing me that it's possible, that's something that I will forever be grateful to Malini for.

Sonal @pinkpeppercorn_sonal

In 2015, when I told my mom that I wanted to start blogging, she showed me a page called MissMalini. And she said, 'If you want to become a blogger, then here's who you should aim to be like.' I actually met Malini in 2021 and got to know her personally! And I realized that what I saw all those many years ago was just the tip of the iceberg! Malini is the kindest, most down to earth and supportive person I've ever met in my life! It was then that I absolutely fell in love with her. She may not even know it, but Malini Agrawal has been one of the most positive influences in my content creation journey and in life in general.

A big congratulations to her on her second book and I'm sure it'll be a huge success!

Vivek Dhadha @vivekdhadha

The first time I met Malini in person was about six years ago, and I distinctly remember how I was in awe of her energy and love for content creation. My own content creation journey has been influenced by her in so many ways—when I was managed by MissMalini's Ignite, or her constant encouragement to create more luxury- and diamond-related content. Till date, I am in awe of her ability to always create meaningful content and always thinking out of the box. Absolute love for this boss lady, and congratulations on her second book. I am sure there is so much more to come!

Zaid Darbar @zaid_darbar

MissMalini is not just a powerhouse of positivity, she is also an inspiration for many of us in the digital space. I remember how she was always available and there to help everyone—all the creators—whenever we needed her. If there is a party or an event, you know what? She's the one to call. Congratulations, MissMalini, on your second book—it's an incredible achievement. Your work truly makes a difference, and I'm so glad to be a part of a community that spreads positivity and kindness. Keep shining your light.

How to Survive and Thrive Online

MALINI AGARWAL

HarperCollins *Publishers* India

First published in India by HarperCollins *Publishers* 2024
4th Floor, Tower A, Building No. 10, DLF Cyber City,
DLF Phase II, Gurugram, Haryana – 122002
www.harpercollins.co.in

2 4 6 8 10 9 7 5 3 1

Copyright © Malini Agarwal 2024

P-ISBN: 978-93-5699-842-1
E-ISBN: 978-93-5699-851-3

The views and opinions expressed in this book are the author's own and the
facts are as reported by her, and the publishers
are not in any way liable for the same.

Malini Agarwal asserts the moral right
to be identified as the author of this work.

All rights reserved. No part of this publication may be reproduced,
stored in a retrieval system, or transmitted, in any form or by any means,
electronic, mechanical, photocopying, recording or otherwise,
without the prior permission of the publishers.

Typeset in 11/14 ElegaGarmnd BT
Manipal Technologies Limited, Manipal

Printed and bound at
Replika Press Pvt. Ltd.

This book is produced from independently certified FSC® paper to ensure
responsible forest management.

To
my big sister, Shalini Agarwal Nemec.
The greatest positive influence(r) in my life!

Thank you for teaching me the power of positive manifestation and always asking for so little while giving so much. (Visit my insta to see what I'm talking about!)
You make the best damn existential bunny filter I have ever seen.
#iykyk
You are my everything. I love you.

Shalini (age twelve years) and I (age six months)

The detailed notes, appendix and sources pertaining to this book are available on the HarperCollins *Publishers* India website. Scan this QR code to access the same.

Contents

A Note to My Readers	xix
1. Talkin' 'Bout My Generation	1
2. My Love Affair with Social Media	17
3. What's Your Internet Personality Type?	25
4. Social Media Legacy	27

MALINI'S INTERNET RULE # 1
Never post something you can't say to someone's face

5. A Thousand Apologies, Thalaiva!	39
6. But First … #letmetakeaselfie	49
7. Why So Mad?: The Anatomy of a Troll	60
8. Surviving Your Fifteen Minutes of Shame	81
9. Ignore No More	97
10. The Art of the Comeback	135

MALINI'S INTERNET RULE # 2
Followers are people too

11. Look Out for Your Followers	143
12. Everyone's an Influencer	153

13. Kindness Is Key — 164
14. A Word on Positive Masculinity — 184

MALINI'S INTERNET RULE # 3
Spark joy (with your next post)

15. Women, Community and the Internet: Malini's Girl Tribe — 193
16. Sparking Joy Online — 200
17. What's the Tea? — 211

Epilogue — 229
Acknowledgements — 231
Notes, Appendix and Sources — 233
Book Cover Credits — 235

A Note to My Readers

Please note: Much like social media, this is meant to be an interactive experience (well, as interactive as books can be). So, I encourage you to keep a pen and your phone handy as you read and make this book your own with scribbles and doodles and enjoy the activities we've inserted between chapters.

Don't forget to take pictures and post them on social media. Tag me so I can share them too because, after all, that's what we do ☺. I mean, if we didn't post it, did it even happen?!

Throughout this book you will find a series of 'Instagrammable prompts'. Wherever you see this icon 📷 you should immediately whip out your phone and post a story. If you tag me, I'll repost it and then we'll both enjoy our dopamine hit till the next notification appears—#everybodywins

📷 **Please use the tags #undertheinfluence and @maliniagarwal so I don't 'miss' you!**

*Insert appropriate 'MissMalini pun here #iykyk

1

Talkin' 'Bout My Generation

Each age, it is found, must write its own books; or rather, each generation for the next succeeding.
—Ralph Waldo Emerson

I'm not trying to cause a big s-s-sensation
(Talkin' 'bout my generation)
I'm just talkin' 'bout my g-g-generation
(Talkin' 'bout my generation)
—The Who

Hi everybody! I'm Malini Agarwal (aka MissMalini). I guess I should begin by explaining *why* I'm writing this book at all (aside from the fact that I signed a two-book deal with HarperCollins India and they've already paid me 😬).

Nobody ever 'taught' me how to use social media. *I think that was a mistake.*

Why, you may ask? Well, because, believe it or not, I have been somebody's accidental troll too (SPOILER ALERT: read on to find out who!), and if it can happen to me, it can surely happen to you. So, I'm going to try and teach you all the things I wish someone had taught me *before* I signed up for my virtual reality.

Consider this your unofficial textbook, 'a dummy's guide to being good online', if you like. One that should, could and *might just* make it into our 'syllabus' one day and, perhaps, somehow help the learning curve for millennia to come (at least, that's the dream!). I'm really hoping that this book will help you millennials, Gen X, Gen Y, Gen Z—or whatever we're calling the TikTok generation (please god, let it not be 'the TikTok generation')—understand the mistakes I've made and the dopamine hits I've chased, because you might have chased them too.

~~~

In fact, let's do a little test, shall we? When was the last time you opened your social media? If the answer is 'at least once a day' then you're guilty as charged. If you're holding your phone right now, wondering if you should story this page or underline that sentence (see, I already did it for you)—perhaps even add a poll for more engagement—then congratulations, you and I, we are the *same*, my friend. Okay now, go ahead and post your story. I'll wait. (Don't forget to tag me!)

In case you're not familiar with the terms for different generations, here's a handy chart that breaks it down for you.[1]

Which Generation Are You?

Generation name	Birth Starts	Birth Ends	Youngest Age Today*	Oldest Age Today*
The Lost Generation, The Generation of 1914	1890	1919	109	134
The Interbellum Generation	1901	1913	111	123
The Greatest Generation	1910	1924	100	114
The Silent Generation	1925	1945	79	99
Baby Boomer Generation	1946	1964	60	78
Generation X (Baby Bust)	1965	1979	45	59
Xennials	1975	1985	39	49
Millennials, Generation Y, Gen Next	1980	1994	30	44
iGen/Gen Z	1995	2012	12	29
Gen Alpha	2013	2025	1	11

(*age if still alive today)

(Apologies to 'the Lost Generation'. Don't shoot the messenger, this is the first result that pops up if you google 'what generation am I?')

Fun Fact: The 'Baby Boomer' generation were known for, well … the baby boom. With the new-found prosperity after World War II, basically *everybody* was 'doing it' (and I don't mean making reels)! But after that, there have been no real or obvious cultural shifts or characteristics, so they went with X, Y and Z for the next generations. Little did they know we'd end up at what *should* be known as Generation AA (an appropriate name since some social media rehab is definitely in order—stay tuned for my OTT show with the working title of 'Social Disconnect' by the way). But, anyway, Neil Howe and William Strauss are credited with coining the term 'millennial' in 1989, when the new millennium was looming.[2]

Can anybody guess what comes next, since they've literally exhausted the alphabet? Don't fret, I googled it for you.

'… *Generation Beta will be born from 2025 to 2039. If the nomenclature sticks, then we will afterwards have Generation Gamma (the children of Generation Alpha) and Generation Delta. But we won't be getting there until the second half of the twenty-first century,*' says social researcher Mark McCrindle.[3] So, there is plenty of time to reflect on the labels!

Here's another quick visual in case that didn't hit home hard enough.[4]

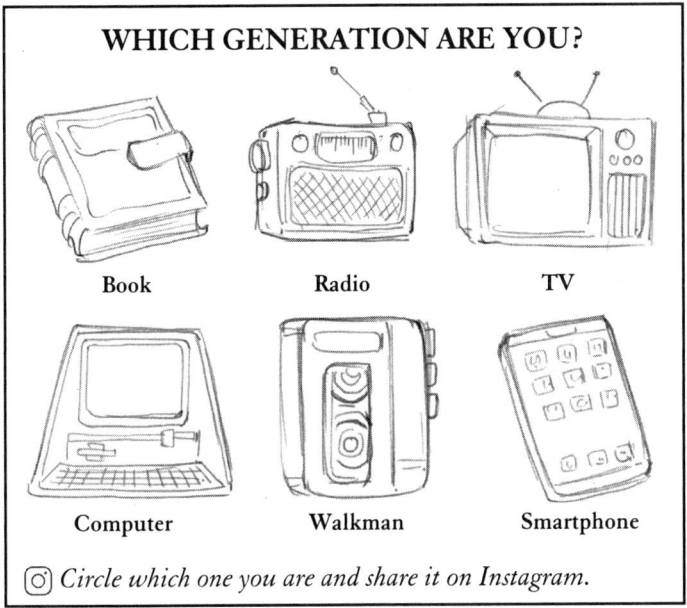

Me? Apparently, I'm a Xennial—forever trapped between Gen X and millennials. Born between 1975 and '85, Xennials are considered a 'microgeneration'.[5]

Perhaps it's worth exploring the differences between Xennials and millennials because it might help you (and me) understand our perspective on things a little better and map out the road ahead. And, while we're at it, let's compare Gen Z and the even more daunting Gen Alpha.

PS: Before Generation Z was decreed the 'official' term, there were a few other candidates, including the 'Selfie Generation'.[6]

Dodged a bullet there, eh, Gen Z?

The Generations	'Gently Does It' Who they are	'It Me' Characteristics	'Generations @ Work' How they work	'Add to Cart' How they shop
Xennials[7] Born: 1975-85	Not digital natives. This gen straddles both the digital and non-digital worlds and understands the importance of both. Most (including myself) didn't have social media through school or college. They have clear memories of their first email address (I'll tell you mine if you tell me yours!), the first games they played online and definitely their first Nokia phone. Because Xennials generally didn't get a cell phone till they were twenty (case in point, I had an alphanumeric pager till I was twenty-two!), they are not dependent on their smartphones.	Physically and mentally active. In spite of having adapted to an increasingly digital world, they are less dependent on smartphones than the next generations. They grew up in a time when technology was advancing fast, but it wasn't nearly as readily available as it is today. Resourceful, logical and good problem-solvers.	Highly adaptive. Equally comfortable learning from a book, blog or podcast. They were born without the internet and yet went on to find online jobs (I felt that #itme).	Some of them have never shopped online and they're okay with that. A luxury marketer's dream, they are affluent and willing to spend on travel for pleasure and on luxury products. Loyal to their brands. Health-conscious.

The Generations	'Gently Does It' Who they are	'It Me' Characteristics	'Generations @ Work' How they work	'Add to Cart' How they shop
Millennials Born: 1980–94	They have an intuitive knowledge of technology, adapt quickly to change and to new and more modernized technology as it becomes available. Most already had MySpace and Facebook and even Orkut. (LOL. Pity Cardi B wasn't around to suggest 'Okurrr'—the platform might have lasted longer!) In 2014, *Time* magazine labelled them the 'me-me-me' generation! (With all due respect and my apologies to millennials, this next analogy is my favourite: 'They spend all the money they should be saving for a house on avocado toast.'[8]	Often labelled lazy, narcissistic and spoilt, they are in fact extremely self-sufficient. They don't need your answers, they can just google it. Confident. Curious. Questioning authority.	Need to feel what they are doing is important. Many millennials grew up with constant praise from their Baby Boomer parents. Evidence: the proverbial millennial 'participation trophy'. Multitasking pros, but also easily distracted, they find social media and texting hard to resist. They do not believe that excessive work demands are worth sacrificing their personal lives. Millennials want flexible work hours and are willing to give up pay increases and promotions for interesting work and a good work-life balance. Like to 'work hard, play harder.'	Professional online shoppers at every turn. Prefer brands that champion transparency and share their values. Millennials in middle and high school were exposed to apparel emblazoned with brand names (I'm looking at you, Ed Hardy). May be willing to pay more for their preferred brands.

The Generations	'Gently Does It' Who they are	'It Me' Characteristics	'Generations @ Work' How they work	'Add to Cart' How they shop
Gen Z Born: 1995–2012	This group is young and has never known a life without tech. They speak tech fluently. Google has always existed for them. They take Wi-Fi for granted. They spend between six and nine hours a day absorbing media. Their preferred mode of communication is digital, primarily through social media and texting. As a group, they could be sitting together in the same restaurant, not talking and yet texting on the same WhatsApp group.	The internet is part of their DNA. It defines how they live, how they learn, how they socialize. Their mastery of technology may make them neglect their interpersonal relationships to a greater extent but they are the ones who give more of a voice to social causes on the internet.	Grew up during the recession of 2022[10] so they're more pragmatic. They want to have a job that provides them a secure personal life. This emerging generation has higher expectations for the workplace than ever before. They prioritize flexible working arrangements, shared values, higher pay, and increased support for mental health. Gen Zers not only know what they want; they are more likely to seek out new opportunities to get it.[11] Preference for traditional communication. Even though Gen Z grew up with texting and instant messages, studies show that they prefer to speak face to face in the workplace.[12]	Attracted to purchases that maximize the value of every buck. Actually *prefer* to shop in stores.[13] Like to feel and see products in person to make sure they're buying something high-quality. Keen on unique experiences that happen in stores (like beauty tutorials, for example).

The Generations	'Gently Does It' Who they are	'It Me' Characteristics	'Generations @ Work' How they work	'Add to Cart' How they shop
Gen Z		They like to get everything they want immediately— insta-food, insta-rides, insta-dates—and their lifestyle is also influenced by YouTubers and social media personalities. In fact, many of them *are* creators themselves. They multitask but their attention span is limited. They are independent and demanding consumers and will have jobs that do not exist in today's world.		Obsessed with finding brands that feel authentic. Don't want to be defined by any brand other than their own. They use social media to find communities where they feel they belong.

The Generations	'Gently Does It' Who they are	'It Me' Characteristics	'Generations @ Work' How they work	'Add to Cart' How they shop
Gen Alpha Born: 2013–25	Alphas will spend all their formative years *totally* immersed in technology. For instance, Prince George of Wales, who is a child, already has an Instagram account (managed by his parents, of course). 'Generation Alpha may simultaneously be growing up faster—or "upaging"—because of their heightened awareness of the world around them, but they've also been cut off from critical in-person social interaction. This has increased their dependence on the technology that has replaced it.'[14]	(It's 2050 picture an usher on a stratospheric balloon ride into outer space in a pressurized space capsule!)[9] Ambitious. Confident. It's hard to tell yet, but the prediction is that this group will be more family-oriented (as their parents will be Gen X and millennials who are particularly engaged as parents and are more digitally savvy than any generation before them). Social researcher Mark McCrindle has an excellent observation to make here:	Fun fact: By 2025, Generation Alpha is expected to be the wealthiest, most educated and technologically literate generation in *history*. As McCrindle says, 'They began being born in 2010, the year the iPad was launched, Instagram was created and App was the word of the year and so have been raised as screenagers to a greater extent than the fixed screens of the past could facilitate.	Used to an excellent online user experience that is seamless and personalized, including cutting-edge ways to interact and communicate. More inclusive and super aware of their (public) image. 'The most important future shoppers can't yet drive [...] The oldest members of the next generation of consumers were born in 2010, yet in just a decade they've learned to become smart online shoppers.

The Generations	'Gently Does It' Who they are	'It Me' Characteristics	'Generations @ Work' How they work	'Add to Cart' How they shop
Gen Alpha		'They are going into a whole new world where we're not labelling as much—we're not saying "they're female and they're male", "they're gay and they're not"... it's becoming more of an open society.'[15] Immersed in technology. Inclusive. High expectations.	For this reason we also call them Generation Glass because the glass that they interact on now and will wear on their wrist, as glasses on their face, that will be on the Head Up Display of the car they learn to drive on, or the interactive school desk where they learn will transform how they work, shop, learn, connect and play.'[16]	In 2020, 81 per cent of children under the age of twelve were reported to influence family purchases, translating to $500 billion in purchases a year. 'Now, with physical retail reopened, they will likely become curious about what brick stores have to offer. This may especially be the case for shopping centers, where many of Gen Alpha's older cohorts, Gen Z, gather to socialize and for a sense of community.'[17]

I wanted to demonstrate the subtle differences between the generations because I want to break the chain of 'I don't understand *this* generation!' An exasperated refrain *every single* generation chimes in with at some critical turning point in time (generally coinciding with the end of its reign). *Cue some ominous *Game of Thrones*, or rather *House of the Dragon*, music here.*

Most importantly, 'understanding each other's views and values will allow different generations to increase their appreciation of one another. This, in turn, will lead to better communication and collaboration because people are now talking from a sense of appreciation and acknowledgement.'[18] And for me that's the rub—how do you elicit the kindness of strangers unless you can understand them? Especially with a vast generational divide, expanding more rapidly than the universe.

By trudging (or trolling) a mile or two in their DMs, perhaps?

The more you think about it, you come to realize everyone who came before the millennials were given a pretty thorough education in offline soft skills. They were often told: 'be courteous and polite', 'don't shout', 'pick up after yourself', 'wait for your turn to speak', 'respect your elders', 'don't show up uninvited', 'don't talk to (creepy) strangers' and, ideally, 'don't *be* a creepy stranger'. In fact, *all* my Xennial friends still echo, *'What's the magic word, beta?'* to their little ones to imprint basic courtesy into their young and impressionable minds.

By the time we grew up, these skills were ingrained in our DNA. But at no point did anyone suggest a similar code of conduct for virtual society. As soon as we travel online, that *entire* education is left at the keyboard. So, everyone jumped online with zero expectations of having to follow any sort of social norms. As a result, millennials and Gen Z—who are still in the process of finding themselves—were exposed to a world of pain and bullying they were never equipped to deal with.

I'm sure you've seen *The Social Dilemma* (2020) by now. One of the most chilling insights I took away from it was spoken by Chamath Palihapitiya, founder and CEO of Social Capital:

> We curate our lives around this perceived sense of perfection because we get rewarded in these short-term signals: hearts, likes, thumbs up and we conflate that with value and we conflate it with truth. And instead, what it is is fake, brittle popularity that's short term and that leaves you even more, and admit it, vacant and empty before you did it. Because that forces you into a vicious cycle where you're like what's the next thing that I need to do now, because I need it back. Think about that compounded by two billion people and then think about how people then react to them to the perceptions of others.[19]

I resonate so hard with this view:

> The dark sides of these online platforms undoubtedly affect us all, but children and younger users are more at risk than the rest of us. The reason for this is simple—this generation of youngsters were born into the social media menace and so have grown to believe that spending several hours of precious time on it as well as the unrealistic portrayals of people and their lives is *normal*. They have little or no point of reference for what life looks or feels like outside their digital villages and so, when that online community seems not to approve of their lives and choices or they're playing a charade that feels inauthentic

to them but is approved by others online (as is often the case), they can spiral easily into an abyss of anxiety and depression.[20]

The game-changer here appears to be the difference in methods of communication. In just three decades, we went from face-to-face relationships to online communities and yet nobody thought to hold up a class (just a *Black Mirror*) to see how things were going. To borrow a phrase from Julia Roberts in *Pretty Woman*, 'Big mistake. HUGE!'

Here are some interesting statistics on trolls that might help demonstrate my point. Two Australian researchers conducted a study to identify certain 'troll traits'. What they discovered was that men were far more likely to become trolls with 'higher levels of psychopathy and sadism'.[21] Sorry guys, but the jury is *in* on this one.

Aside from being men, YouGov, a global public opinion and data company, found that most trolls are on the younger side. Millennials are twice as likely to participate in such behaviour as people aged fifty-five and over.[22] The survey also concluded that 77 per cent of respondents believed anonymity makes people more likely to troll.

A survey conducted by Erin Buckels, assistant professor of psychology (social-personality area) and her colleagues from the university, showed that, across all participants, the average amount of time they admitted devoting to commenting was over an hour a day.[23] Commenting frequency was associated with younger age, being male and high scores on the authors' Global Assessment of Internet Trolling (GAIT) test.

So, while we were racing into the digital age, we, as a species, completely forgot to add an important aspect to our curriculum:

how to behave online. We just never stopped to update the map when it came to crucial things like emotional, intellectual and social preparedness for:

- When you have unfettered access to the entire world at your fingertips—across borders, race, religion, culture, etc.
- Accountability even with anonymity (aka having a conscience)
- Resisting the urge to virtual-vomit every thought that crosses your mind
- Some semblance of virtual law and order/civic sense

Of course, some people are beyond redemption in this regard. Many trolls are, in fact, trolls in real life. Sick f*cks like the creators of the Blue Whale Challenge[24]—an online game that involved manipulating young children into hurting themselves and even led to death by suicide—could only be the work of a clinical sadist.

But since we've given literally everyone with an internet connection free entry into our minds, surely a little governance is in order? A digital reimagining of social ethics? Perhaps even a 'troll police' that issues a kind of certificate of sanity, conducts a quick background check that gives you a unique virtual visa (that can be traced back to you), with repeat offenders being denied access to digital society, just like we put criminals in real-life in jail? I know we have cyber laws and stuff but I have yet to test their effectiveness in battling the continuous barrage of verbal assault that women face online on a daily basis. (In fact, there's an interesting experiment I did on this, so stay tuned for DMing my creepy DMers, further along in this book.)

Since all this appears to still be a major work in progress (with the many layers of conflict it may stir up within a democracy), perhaps it would help to start at the beginning and offer a little self-help for parents to guide their children, and to equip us with tools to handle trolling without causing significant damage to our mental health and, perhaps, even for trolls to learn how to 'un-troll'.

So let's see, where do I begin. *How* do I teach anyone to be 'good' online?

If, by the way, you're looking for a crash course in social media, internet hacks and becoming an influencer, you're one book too late. Please help yourself to a copy of my first one, *#tothemoon: How I Blogged My Way To Bollywood*, where I literally spell out the A to Z of building a personal digital brand (and incorporating shameless plugs seamlessly into conversation.) Then come back to this one—or actually, read this first. It's always good to start with a conscience; it'll hurt less later.

2

My Love Affair with Social Media

> *If you are on social media and you are not learning, not laughing, not being inspired or not networking, then you are using it wrong.*
> —Germany Kent

Truth be told, social media used to be a kinder place.

Let me tell you about my first brush with social media. Back in November 1996, I was introduced to a cross-platform instant messaging and VoIP (Voice over Internet Protocol) client called ICQ, a clever phonetic derivation of the phrase 'I seek you'. I'm sorry to say that innocent little flower icon that I grew to know and love, and the 'uh-oh!' notification sound that used to be my straight hit of dopamine before I knew the word even existed, would never pass the vibe check today!

But a twenty-something 'Miss' Malini decided to make BFFs with a complete stranger who called himself 'Wildthing'—and I kid you not, we are still friends today, twenty-seven years later! Now, the chances of you or I befriending a fellow called 'Wildthing' in this day and age, and living to tell the tale, would be slim to none (also, my handle was ababecalledmanzil, so I'm not allowed to judge—long story, read the first book—and so I guess they both deserved each other). My point is that the true beauty of that friendship lay in the fact that—and I truly believe this—Karan Chopra (albeit under the guise of a questionable username like Wildthing, which he insists I mention was inspired by Steppenwolf) was still digitally incorrupt and socially well-conditioned enough to behave in a respectable manner with a total stranger purely based on his prior upbringing. And for that I am grateful, or we wouldn't still be friends two-and-a-half decades later—it would have been dick pic and done.

I asked KC what his thoughts on social media are some decades later and what code of conduct he was following as a male on the internet back in '96, and this is what he had to say.

KC says ...

So, first of all, Malini, let me set the record straight-ish. It was 'Wildthing' because of Steppenwolf's only hit song that we were all singing with our cool personalized air guitars because it was the '90s and we actually had a TV to watch and have deep cultural learnings from. A sharp contrast to the '80s, when we had *Krishi Darshan* to watch and static 'off times' when Doordarshan was resting. The hunger for all things international was high and Americana was abounding in its full glory, given the '80s were really an American decade globally. At the end of that line, when we were sufficiently immersed in MTV and in love with several video jockeys at the same time, came this thing called the dial-up internet.

Okay boys, you want a connection ... with the Playboy channel? Or 'the one with the Playboy channel,' an aged relative enquired one fine day. Lunch ended at that moment as far as we were concerned. A very impatient and feverish week later, a friend of mine had a bonafide MTNL dial modem installed on his super-fast, latest on-fire Pentium I desktop, politely and patiently assembled by a man claiming to be a student of computer science from IIT. He had the 'Playboy' connection, which was the term for 'faster' internet, or premium paid connection, that actually loaded images on your screen—get this—in colour. *Mind blown*! Now the relatively poor (me) among us hadn't the slightest idea on how to get this connection at home just yet. So, we did what everyone 'in the know' did. We brib@# (can't really confess to that here) ... er ... requested someone in charge to help us with any usernames or passwords of people who may have gotten a connection and didn't really use or 'need' them—in case any such information tripped and fell into my screen. This was a small club of a few thousand people, at least in South Delhi—but more importantly, an entire demographic got online on this. A great example of how a boom blossomed with little or no regulation at the time. I don't think we would have been able to afford any organized regulations that early in the digital revolution: I guess that's how it became a revolution, spreading everywhere—someone could just plug a modem into a computer. We were all similar people with access to a computer and we wanted to know what the hell we could do with this machine. I, for one, had come into this whole thing to play video games. If I hadn't loved those games, I'd probably be illiterate today or have a real job, who knows?

So, here we are, with this just in, and then comes ICQ. I'm sure you can conjure up those two sounds in your head, the dial up and that 'uh-oh' from ICQ's little applet. As a male and as a teenager (I think that was it), there was no precedence of behaviour really, so the majority of people coming online with the attitude of 'great effort, expense and enthusiasm' were a curious bunch. This was no utopia but a majority of people online and seeking contact with the world assumed, I guess, that the person on the other end was just like them. The prerequisites were quite common: you had to be good with the English language, you needed an address and a phone line, you were not personally liable for what you say and could log off when you came across a weirdo, because 'So what?' or 'Kya kar lega?' The virtual was truly virtual and most gatekeepers had no clue what we were doing online.

I think my generation connected with each other and all over the world for the first time. The whole eccentric 'pen friend' concept was transformed and now you had ICQ buddies. Geeks like me, who in those days had less schoolfriends, suddenly were chatting with people who 'would not be seen dead with you' in real life. So, there was no code but there were unspoken rules of engagement that people took very seriously. You could cut off someone abruptly (yes, ghost effectively) and that would lead to a great amount of frustration because the idea of an online identity or privacy was not really a thing, at least in my South Delhi-based memory. Privacy was easier to manage.

ababecalledmanzil could've been an alien luring young and beautiful men for 'dinner', a large, middle-aged man with a taxidermy collection and a pet lizard or even a serial killer. Initially, I did suspect she was one of these because her gender at the time wasn't so friendly to the geek. So, I put her through my 'test'. You want to know about that test? That's cute but I'm not telling, ever.

ICQ became the explosion point for what would become social media; it was everything you wanted it to be, a dark portal to buy suspect items from suspect strangers, a meeting point for old friends living far away, a dating portal—and it opened my world to a lot of new people. You kept it 'cool' and tried to keep your friend list relevant and hip. No relatives were welcome; it was counterculture at its best. We suddenly had a channel to show one another all that the '90s gave us culturally through finding like-minded people and creating an online community (cue heavenly music) ... aaaand then it got very weird very fast ☺. 'Manzil' became 'Malini', and I became 'KC'. Almost all of the rest of my chat list had to be erased and then fumigated a few times before I bowed out of ICQ (yay) ... and ... joined Orkut. HUGE FACEPALM!'

LOL, Orkut! Yes, I do recall. But by then the innocence of that erstwhile South Delhi–Mayur Vihar IC-cuteness was long gone already. I bet you're dying to see what we looked like back in the day, right? I had a feeling, so here you go.

So, what have we lost? I believe Gen Z and Alpha have been robbed of the golden opportunity to use the internet for healthy social interaction in a way that would have deeply enriched their lives and expanded their horizons. Now, we're all just sitting here horrified at how 'toxic' the internet can be. But as my friend Rij Eappen aka @kingofclubsin often reminds me, we keep complaining about this 'toxic internet' or 'toxic social media' but it's not some alien nation that showed up and now we have to deal with it. We *are* social media: we invented it; every word, gesture and action that is on it has been created by us. So, maybe, we need to step back and detoxify some peeps before this online creep-culture penetrates our offline reality too. Who's to stop someone from turning up unannounced at our door or dropping their pants in public if we keep giving them a free pass to do it online?

There is a hilarious but totally terrifying experiment that went all kinds of wrong that demonstrates how artificial intelligence (AI) may not be the villain of this movie after all. In 2016, it took less than twenty-four hours for Twitter (now known as X) to corrupt an innocent AI chatbot. Microsoft unveiled Tay, a Twitter bot that the company described as an experiment in 'conversational understanding'. The more you chat with Tay, said Microsoft, the smarter it gets, learning to engage people through 'casual and playful conversation'.[25] Unfortunately, the conversations didn't stay playful for long. Pretty soon after Tay launched, people started tweeting at the bot with all sorts of misogynistic, racist and Donald Trump-ist remarks. And Tay—being essentially a robot parrot with an internet connection—started repeating these sentiments back to users. It's a joke, obviously, but it raised serious questions, including: how are we going to teach AI using public data without incorporating the worst traits of humanity?

I heard an epic podcast recently which unpacked how Elon Musk's early stage 'Twitter addiction' quite possibly, single-handedly rewrote the future of X the podcast says. 'The experience on social media of speaking to an audience larger than just the people you know, it's like walking out on your balcony and then just loudly saying something. It's awkward, as you wait then to see if a crowd will gather, laugh or applaud. But the first time it does happen for you, if it does happen, is a transcendent time, better than many drugs. 2011 was when Elon Musk may have first learned to love that balcony high; that was also the last year of his life where he was not a billionaire. And at a time when, well he may have been well-known in some circles, even well regarded, he was not yet anywhere near being one of the internet's main characters.'[26] So maybe we need to learn a thing or two ourselves before we teach ChatGPT anything else.

3

What's Your Internet Personality Type?

> *The most important kind of freedom is to be what you really are.*
> —Jim Morrison

Take this Mashable quiz to find out your personality type.

https://mashable.com/article/online-personality-quiz/.[27]

My results were eerily accurate. I'm what's known as PSDO (Peacemaker, Sharer, Distracted, Offline). Here are my results.

> **Peacemaker**: You do not believe in fighting online, so you don't do it. Your mentions are probably gorgeous and empty, like the Grand Canyon or an antique vase. You see the word 'beef' and probably just think of meat. Congrats, you.
>
> **Sharer**: It's likely that you have little to no trepidation of sharing your life online. You have nothing to hide. And if someone doesn't like your post? They can unfollow you. You may or may not care about this part.
>
> **Distracted**: You can't focus on one thing online for very long, but who can blame you? There are so many versions of the Distracted Boyfriend meme to analyze. Sure, you might have tried the SelfControl app before, but eighth time's the charm.
>
> **Offline**: You have definitely tweeted something you thought you were typing in the search bar, and you probably don't have the two-factor authentication. You might not spend much time online at all. Instead, you have IRL hobbies. You probably don't have a Vitamin D deficiency. Nice!

◉ Take the quiz and share your results!

4

Social Media Legacy

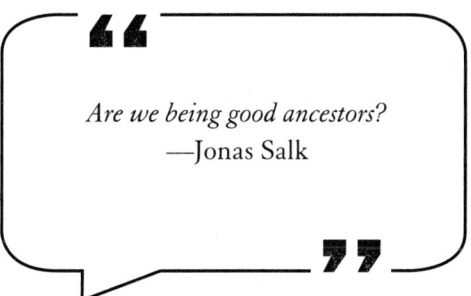

Are we being good ancestors?
—Jonas Salk

Okay, so you get it, a little Social Media Netiquette 101 couldn't possibly hurt. In fact, it might make a nice IRL (in real life) gift for the kids on their birthdays over Zoom. But, you might still be wondering, why should you listen to *me*? Who am I to wax eloquent about how you should behave online? The answer is actually pretty boring. Because, honestly, my friend, I've been doing this for a *very* long time and I have learned the very long and very hard way. So, I'm here offering you a fast pass to redemption. Enjoy.

To put this in context, I started my blog before most people in India were even on social media (*before* TikTok and Snapchat, just around the same time as Netflix actually but before it was a thing to 'Netflix and chill'). In my time as an 'influencer', I've worked with every single major social media platform—some right from when they started—and I've witnessed the social media experience from both sides, the people and the platforms. I've come to realize that social media may be broken and we're the only ones who can fix it, seeing as how we're the ones who broke it in the first place. So, for the next 200 pages (or swipes if you're on your Kindle) I'd like you to try and 'unlearn' the internet with me.

But I'm getting ahead of myself. First, let me take you back to where social media began for me.

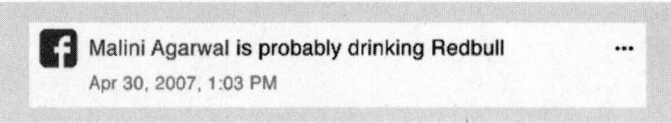

(Yup, if you know me, in some ways, not much has changed.)

Stage 1: Facebook!

Remember the time when Facebook was all about posting these witty one-liner 'status updates'? You just had to fill in the blank: *Malini is ... something.* And, *of course,* I would try and think of the cleverest thing (or so I thought at the time). Here are a few of my classics:

> **f** Malini Agarwal is ready to take over the world. ···
> Aug 6, 2007, 1:09 PM
>
> **f** Malini Agarwal is winning at LIFE! ···
> May 14, 2007, 1:09 PM
>
> **f** Malini Agarwal is humming out of tune. ···
> May 8, 2007, 2:58 PM
>
> **f** Malini Agarwal is not quite sure what her status is today. ···
> Apr 30, 2007, 1:03 PM

*The last was one of my favourites and Timehop tells me that was fifteen years ago.

Back then, I felt this weird *excitement* that all my friends, and some random acquaintances, would read these and think I'm so clever, so *cool*. Virtual life was fun. I could send my friends virtual gifts, find old boyfriends just to see how awful they looked after a few years (you've done it too, admit it #stalkedanexonfacebook) and share my fabulous life (or at least just the parts that looked fabulous) with the entire world—in an instant.

So yeah, I drank the Kool-Aid. I was *obsessed*. I'd post pictures of *everything* I did, in real time. And suddenly my world was populated with everyone whose names or faces I could remember. Amazing, right?

And then came Stage 2: Twitter ... (aka the artist formerly known as Twitter, now just an ominous X thanks to Elon Musk)

I remember I was at a bar in Mumbai called Ghetto, and Rohit Gupta, a friend I used to play pool with, came up to me and casually said, 'Hey, Malini, have you heard of Twitter? I think you will like it ...' I went home, made my Twitter account and posted asking people to follow my blog ...

And BOOM!

I had started a real-time dialogue with the *entire* world in twenty seconds. This was not just a one-way conversation. It was an actual *dialogue*.

Have you ever thought about how people communicated in the past? Without phones or fax machines or email? The ancient Greek messenger Philippides (530–490 BC) ran a distance of about 250–300 kms in two–three days and then ran back. He ran from Athens to Sparta and then to Marathon and finally back to Athens to announce the victory of the Greeks over the Persians.[28] That's intense. In fact, just about twenty years ago, you had to wait *three weeks* for a reply to your painstakingly written snail mail (if you were Salman Khan, you had to train his kabutar to '*Jaa jaa jaa*' and deliver his '*pehli pyaar ki pehli chitthi*'). But now I had this amazing superpower to communicate instantly with anyone … even though I didn't really know what I was supposed to do with it.

It felt like being in a virtual living room, like walking around having various, simultaneous conversations with people I'd never met, but without that awkward introduction of 'Who are you? What do you do? What are you doing here? Who invited you?'. I could dive right in. No security check and no invitation required. This magical ability of communicating with more people than otherwise humanly possible, by typing 140 characters and hitting send, blew my mind.

And then came Instagram. To which I was late by a whole year! If you remember, the first time Instagram launched it was only available on iOS, for iPhone users. I couldn't get Instagram because I didn't have an iPhone and I even started a 'Malini needs an iPhone' campaign with little success. Eventually, of course, Instagram went Android and my Insta-FoMO was alleviated.

But *why* do I love social media so much? This tool could amplify your ability to connect with people on a scale that is not otherwise humanly possible. I can have 5,000 friends on Facebook (odd cut-off point, btw) and connect with them at different times about different things but I can never keep up that number of relationships in real life.

The fact is, there are proper scientific reasons as to why we're so hooked to social media.

What the brain 'Likes'

When millions wake up and tweet about the weather, Instagram their breakfast or send a Snapchat, they're getting one undeniable benefit: *brain candy* (emphasis mine).

In 2010, researchers found that 80 per cent of social media posts were announcements about people's immediate experiences—Facebook status updates like Joe's 'OMG that is A LOT of snow' are the norm on social feeds. So in 2012, two researchers at Harvard were curious about this and decided to see how self-disclosure affects the brain.

> It turns out that talking about our own thoughts and experiences activates the rewards system of the brain, providing that same shot of dopamine we get from sex, food and exercise. The reward activity in the brain is also much greater when people get to share their thoughts with others.

Simply put, your wake-up tweets give your brain *pleasure*.[29]

There's a quote from a movie called *Shall We Dance?* (average movie but epic quote!) that has stayed with me for years. It goes: 'There are six billion [make that seven billion now] people on the planet, what does one life really mean? In marriage or friendship you're saying I'm going to be there for the good, the bad, the mundane, your life will not go unnoticed because I will notice it, your life will not go unwitnessed because I will be your witness.'

And what else is social media other than a witness? A like, a share, a double tap on Instagram—it's somebody acknowledging your existence, being your witness, saying that your life matters without saying that your life matters. That's why we love it.

But have you ever stopped to think: *What am I making them witness? And what kind of witness am I being?*

My entire career started with a blog back in 2008 but it really blew up when social media took over our consciousness. When I started my blog, I was a straight-up Bollywood gossip blogger and I loved it! Looking back, I'm not proud of everything I've posted. In fact, a few crucial things happened that made me rethink being a gossip blogger.

Gradually, I started feeling wary of running into certain celebrities at events because of what we had written. That's when it dawned on me that the virtual world had given me a free pass to behave in a way I would *never* have done in person. Suddenly, I was hurting people I didn't even know for a few clicks, trying to raise my social clout with the number of followers or likes I had. Who had I become? And why? Was it just greed for social currency or something else?

If I knew then what I know now, I would probably have thought very differently about what I posted. But how could I have known the future? Social media was a free-for-all platform. Sign up, log in, do your worst. While growing up, we were educated in the things that are now second nature to us: how to walk, talk, eat, *behave*. We were taught right from wrong. We were taught subjects—English, math, sciences—that would equip us to deal with the world when we were adults.

Think about it, if I gave you the keys to my car and never taught you how to drive, you'd probably crash it, right? Or imagine if in biology class, I handed you a frog and a scalpel with zero instructions …

Who remembers this game, btw?

Frog in a Blender was created by Joe Cartoon, and it was all the rage back in 2007. Since then, it has been downloaded around 110 million times. Frankly, this should have been our first warning of what's to come on the internet. People getting a kick out of digitally blending a frog till he literally explodes—that should have been a red flag right there.

So why were we *never* taught how to use social media?

I guess you'd expect that people would use their judgement and behave online the same as they did in real life, with basic politeness and socially acceptable behaviour. We all know that didn't happen. But why?

You know what, I'm as guilty as the next person of getting social media wrong. So, let me take you through my social media legacy and share with you the lessons I've learnt along the way.

We really are in Neo's 'matrix' in a sense. The future we keep talking about is *now*. We may not have the flying cars to prove it but we're here. We're in it. Maybe we just don't know how to live here yet. That's when I made my first rule about internet usage.

And now begins a social media guide on how to be 'good' on the internet in three parts. Hope you enjoy the ride!

MALINI'S INTERNET RULE # 1

Never post something you can't say to someone's face

5

A Thousand Apologies, Thalaiva!

> *You make mistakes, mistakes don't make you.*
> —Maxwell Maltz

Back in 2008, I got some pictures of Rajinikanth without his hair and makeup on. I assumed since people love to see candid pictures of stars in Hollywood, I thought nothing about it and posted them. The next day, I woke up to a flurry of angry messages from fans. They weren't trolling me. They were genuinely upset and angry about what I had done to their idol. And that's when it hit me.

We talk about fat shaming and complexion shaming, but what had I done? *I had shamed the man too.*

That morning, I asked myself this: If there were no likes or no public display of the number of my 'followers', would I still use social media the same way? And what does that say about me?

I deleted the post and wrote an apology. But here's the thing. The more I thought about it, the more it made me wonder what gave rise to that kind of behaviour. Is it just because we opened ourselves up to too many people too fast? Or is it something about the medium and the anonymity it affords that tips people over to the dark side?

I once had a conversation about human behaviour, karma and how we interact in the real world and it struck me that it has (over centuries and perhaps right from the very beginning of time) been perfectly normal behaviour to walk into a room full of *other humans* and show no sign of greeting or even acknowledgement that they even exist. And then I started wondering if the same is true for animals. Like, do cows stand around in a field in little cliques of their own? Do they know the other cows around them or do they just passive-aggressively coexist, with zero f*cks to give about each other? This particular epiphany of mine happened while talking to a Frenchman who was in India for the first time, representing the global team from Moet & Chandon. As he smiled and nodded politely, it occurred to me that I had somehow brought up cows and reincarnation in a conversation while professing that I was Hindu but not a very religious one! Well played, Malini, well played.

The reason I'm telling you this story is because it made me think about how differently we behave online than we do off it. In real life, there are some unspoken boundaries and limits to the liberties you can take with other people's space. Boundaries that don't quite seem to have made a map online. For example, I would never go up to a total stranger and poke them in the ribs (circa Facebook 2007) just like you wouldn't shove an eggplant (or the organ it resembles) in someone's face to say hello (or at least, that's the hope).

Since this is a fun reimagining of the game 'Never Have I Ever', the quiz below has more examples. But my point is this: why did the basic guidelines of socially acceptable behaviour evaporate as soon as we lost our physical form? Is the theatre of our minds just that degenerated or are we simply missing a few facts?

The Never Have I Ever Quiz

How to play: Tick mark or circle everything you've never done. You are your own witness, don't cheat. *Because Rahul is a cheater and you are not.*

Never Have I Ever: Social Media Edition

(Circle everything you've NEVER done.)

Slid into someone's DMs unprovoked	Taken a screenshot of a private conversation and sent it to someone else	Posted a 'thirst trap'	Done a follower/following clean-up because it was starting to feel vapid
DMed a celebrity crush	Shared my Insta password with a friend	Deleted a social media account because of trolls	Checked a notification while driving
Blocked/reported a troll	Put a raw, unfiltered photo on my feed	Put a lock on my social media to minimize screen time	Compared myself to others online
Made a public profile private	Asked for the price and then ghosted an online seller because it was too expensive	Had thumb ache from holding the phone for too long	Sulked because I didn't get the likes I expected
Dropped my phone on my face while I was in bed	Got inspired by a celeb/influencer to buy/try something	Searched for an ex on social media	Regretted putting up a photo and then archived it

Instagram story template by @maliniagarwal

Now, take a picture and post it on your Instagram stories and nominate five friends to do the same.

While scrolling through the comments on my Instagram account, I often wonder how perfectly common it is for someone to post a reply that has absolutely *nothing* to do with the post itself. For example, I posted a question about having writer's block one day and solicited some help by asking these three questions:

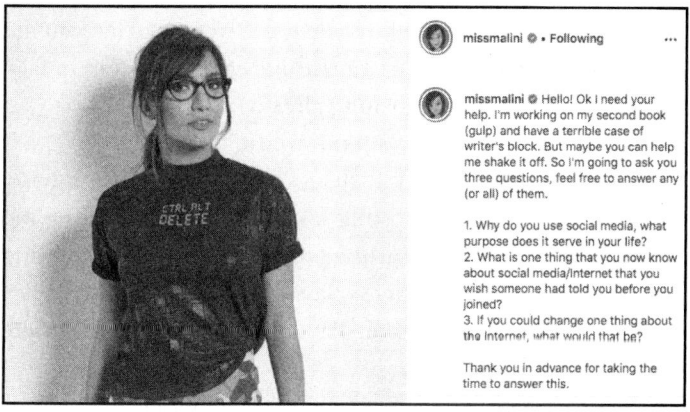

At least two people used this as an opportunity to ask for a #follow4follow, others dropped a series of fire emojis (which I'm guessing had more to do with the picture than appreciation for my question), someone told me I'm 'very beautiful looking' (I'll take it!) and yet another used this real estate to offer life-changing predictions via an astrological hotline.

Imagine this scenario in a real-life setting. A bunch of people popping into a conversation to say the most random, unrelated things and bounce, leaving behind a muddy flier on the floor of your reality. Yet, this is completely par for the course online.

So much so that we simply ignore it, just as we would a drunk in real life.

How did we get here? Because surely all these people *also* live in the real world? They can't possibly be exhibiting this behaviour IRL.

All of us think of ourselves as 'good people' but does our social media reflect that? Have all the comments you've made on social media indicated that? Or have you been an accidental troll like me sometimes?

The thing is, right now, there is no accountability for our online behaviour. But what if there were? What if what you did on social media had significant real-life consequences? In fact, in some countries it's happening already!

China has started a 'social credit' system—the exact methodology is a secret but things like bad driving, buying too many video games, posting fake news online, posting too much on social media or surfing porn are punished by banning offenders from buying business class train tickets or flying! They are also rewarding people for having a good score with more matches on dating sites.[30]

Let's be honest, if *your* social media footprint were investigated like they do in China, ask yourself, would *you* be able to fly?

Really think about this: If you swapped virtual reality with 'reality' reality, what kind of a person would you be? Would you really behave the same way? What would you change? In order to demonstrate this, let's imagine social media is a virtual version of an *actual* party.

Would you go around taking Polaroid pictures of yourself and hand them out to everyone?

Would you double tap people's faces and walk away?

Would you point at the host and loudly say how ugly her dress is?

Would you just drop your pants to say hi?!

I hope the answer to all of the above is no.

So then *why* do we treat the internet like a dumping ground for all our negative emotions? And never for a second think about the fact that everything we post is a reflection of ourselves and it's going to be there *forever*, like plastic?

Just imagine your kids googling you one day. Is there something you wish they never see? Chances are, they will.

And I suppose that was my first epiphany. When I prepared for my TEDx NMIMS talk on social media legacy, I literally tallied up everything I had ever put out online. Including the number of tweets, Facebook posts, etc., and everything else and asked myself the all-important question: just because space on the internet or social media is limitless, does that mean I should be less mindful of the crap I'm hoarding there?

Or, more simply put, do I regret anything I've said online? The answer, dear Rajinikanth, is a resounding yes and I'm willing to admit you weren't the first or last victim of my oblivion. I just didn't realize I was being part of the problem because it was on the internet, and the *internet has no rules*.

I started as a Bollywood blogger, so considering people's 'feelings' was never part of the job description. I was, I thought, just following in the footsteps of our cigarette-wielding Madam M (and her Cleopatra-esque black cat) of *Filmfare* lore and she didn't seem at all apologetic or bothered by it. You know why? Because *anonymity is your ticket out of accountability and THAT is the problem with the internet*. While I was the cute anime Miss 'M' that many didn't realize is a real human being (some even to this day don't), it was all fun and games. But you really start hitting the *feels* when both parties realize the other one is human. Because then you start to (rightfully) expect a little humanity.

> *John Hobbes: Can I ask you a personal question?*
> *Gretta Milano: Everything is personal, if you're a person.*
> —Fallen, *1998*

That's when the penny dropped, I guess, and I was sure *I* for one would know where to draw the line. My moral compass was now fully tuned. I would think first and blog later. So now I'm set, right? Wrong.

I learned another very important lesson some years later when I first met Ranveer Singh in 2011 at the Blender's Pride Fashion Tour. I was super thrilled to see him for the first time and went bouncing up to him to say hello. But he said, 'MissMalini, I'm really mad at you!' I was shocked and exclaimed, 'Why?!', to which he drew my attention to a blog that a member of my team had written mocking his rap on *India's Most Desirable* (a highly ironic act considering the legendary success of *Gully Boy* a decade later, I realize). And my first reaction was a defensive 'But I didn't even write that post!' But the fact is, if it went up on my blog, I had to take accountability for it. So, I apologized and he was super gracious about it all although I could tell we had really hurt his feelings and that was certainly never my intention. So, I shared a simple rule with my entire team.

When in doubt about whether to carry a piece of 'juicy gossip' or write an opinion about someone, celebrity or otherwise, ask yourself this: Would you feel comfortable saying it to their face? That is, do you have the balls for the eyeballs? And if the answer is no then you cannot write it at all. That is the rule we've stood by for the last decade and a half.

Obviously, for me, there were repercussions to that. Tabloids are notorious for their scoops and 'blind items'. I completely stopped doing them, retired the MissMalini 'fashion police' and stuck to the happy shiny quadrant. So, of course people assumed I was sucking up to Bollywood celebrities. I didn't get every juicy scoop out like everyone else. In fact, 80 per cent of the 'gossip' I know, I will never tell anyone, and I'm okay with that.

Once, I was replying to a really mean comment online and I asked, genuinely (and somewhat exasperated), 'Why did you need to be so mean about it?' The response I got was, 'What do you expect, this is the internet.' That's when it hit me that something was terribly wrong with how we were behaving online. We desperately need to unlearn this version of the internet, where we have lost all empathy and kindness. We must reboot.

PS: What a great self-check, right? Next time, before you post or comment, ask yourself, 'Would I say this in real life?' You'll be surprised by how differently you may respond.

6

But First … #letmetakeaselfie

> *The camera cannot lie, but it can be an accessory to untruth.*
> —Harold Evans

I want to begin by asking a simple question. Who offered everyone this internet 'free pass' or, more importantly, who started it? What is it about the internet that makes this kind of fish-market-y (inventing words is allowed on the internet, okay!?) so prevalent?

I came across a fascinating podcast while writing this book. It's called *The Secret History of the Future*, hosted by *The Economist*'s Tom Standage and Seth Stevenson of *Slate*.[31] It blew my mind in so many different ways. I highly recommend you listen to it. The premise of the podcast is that if you delve far back into the past, you'll eventually unlock a few secrets about the future. Because—as we all know—history repeats itself and, as per the hosts, 'discovering how people reacted to past innovations can also teach us about our [future] selves'. Interesting.

Here's what really piqued my interest. In the podcast, the hosts share the story of an anthropologist, Ted Carpenter, who, in 1969, decided to conduct an experiment with the people of Papua New Guinea. The people had never seen themselves in a picture before (some not even in a mirror). Carpenter's goal was to see what impact a mirror or the image of oneself had on the people. The result was pretty chilling.

'So these people went from zero to "selfie" in just a few seconds and it kind of blew their minds and they started almost immediately helping the camera to tell lies,' says Stevenson. Of course, it took them a minute to understand what was going on; Mr Carpenter had to point to their noses or hair and the corresponding parts in the picture for it to sink in. 'Once they understood that they could see their soul, their image, their identity outside of themselves, they were startled.'[32]

Read that sentence again and tell me you didn't get goosebumps! Instagram much? Mr Carpenter called this phenomenon 'instant alienation', which made the self, more real, more dramatic and, I suppose, more alone. Eventually, they started wearing these photos of themselves on their foreheads, almost like a second face. And their friends would greet them by first looking at the photo and presumably making some kind of judgement. *The photo becomes the more important manifestation.*

This brought up an interesting and somewhat eerie point. In today's digital age, we see each other on social media far more than we do in real life. Think about it, think about all the people you know (maybe aside from your immediate family or work colleagues whom you may see every day), and now think about how often you've seen your friends in person compared to how many times you've seen them on social media in any given week. What impact does that have on you? Which version of them do you know better? Which version do you most associate with them? Pictures have a way of carving a permanent memory in our minds, even if it's a falsehood. That's the entire basis of a memory trick called 'the mind palace':

> A mind or memory palace is an imaginary location in your mind where you can store mnemonic images. The most common type of memory palace involves making a journey through a place you know well, like a building or town. Along that journey there are specific locations that you always visit in the same order.[33]

Social media has only been around for fifteen years or so, which is why Stevenson says, 'I don't think we've fully come to grips with how that is changing us.' The photo is becoming the identity, not unlike a Polaroid picture on the forehead, and somehow that has become more important. So now we're trapped in this little image of ourselves that we want people to associate with us. A long stream of images, in fact, with which we are piecing together our curated identity.

Somewhere along the way I had started thinking about the virtual world as an alternate reality. A 'second life', if you will. You know, when you think about it, you realize how we're all basically living in Season 3, Episode 1 of *Black Mirror*: 'Nosedive'. If you haven't seen it, please stop reading immediately, watch it and come back. I'll wait.

> Taking a photograph has been pretty effortless for some time now. But what has changed? According to Standage and Stevenson, it is that we now have a social network to share it on. An impulse to share means we're now seeing the photo with a potential audience in mind, instead of based on our own instinct. We're using our photos to communicate, we're using our pictures to talk, like a language. Snapchat's disappearing images, for instance, are meant to reflect real-life conversations, which is why their pictures disappear real-time and aren't meant to be revisited and examined, liked or shared at some later point.

Now that you are suitably spooked, let's continue!

The App Trap and FoMO

However, it's not totally our fault. Today, apps are designed to have a huge impact on us. They encourage infinite scrolling, becoming slaves to the elusive algorithm, an insatiable greed for digital currency in likes and follows and then some and, of course, give us FoMO!

> Fear of missing out (FoMO) is a unique term introduced in 2004 and then extensively used since 2010 to describe a phenomenon observed on social networking sites. It eventually made it to the Oxford dictionary in 2013. In 2013, British psychologists elaborated and defined it as 'pervasive apprehension that others might be having rewarding experiences from which one is absent', FoMO is characterized by the desire to stay continually connected with what others are doing [...] The conceptualization that FoMO involves negative affect from unmet social needs is similar to theories about the negative emotional effects of social ostracism. FoMO is a relatively new psychological phenomenon. It may exist as an episodic feeling that occurs in mid-conversation, as a long-term disposition, or a state of mind that leads the individual to feel a deeper sense of social inferiority, loneliness, or intense rage. Today, more than ever, people are exposed to a lot of details about what others are doing; and people are faced with the continuous uncertainty about whether they are doing enough or if they are where they should be in terms of their life. FoMO includes two processes; firstly, perception of missing out, followed up with a compulsive behavior to maintain these social connections

> [...] FoMO is considered as a type of problematic attachment to social media, and is associated with a range of negative life experiences and feelings, such as a lack of sleep, reduced life competency, emotional tension, negative effects on physical well-being, anxiety and a lack of emotional control; with intimate connections possibly being seen as a way to counter social rejection. In the last seven years, research has been done to establish its links with various mental health outcomes.[34]

FoMO ran deep in our collective consciousness as we strode into a twenty-first century full of soaring work stress and burgeoning social media. Patrick McGinnis, entrepreneur, angel investor and author, and the man behind the first FoMO meme, says it has always existed, but not in such a personal way: 'Thanks to laptops and mobile phones, we now carry our lives around with us as never before. When I started at Harvard Business School in 2002 there was a Perfect Storm for FoMO.'[35]

Patrick also coined FoBO btw. 'Fear of a Better Option' implicitly assumes that you will have better options from which you might be able to choose at some point in the future (With FoMO you mainly hurt yourself, while FoBO is about being fundamentally selfish when it comes to relationships).[36] And then came JoYO (Joy of Missing Out), FoBI (Fear of Being Invited) and my personal kryptonite, FoGO (coined by my friend Sushil Charmes, Fear of Getting Over). I legit sometimes suffer a deep sadness at the beginning of a day I have been looking forward to because I am critically aware that it will soon be over—even if that 'soon' is twelve hours away. Yes, I need help, but for now, let's move on! (You only have 166 pages left.

Who knows, you might feel some JoGO (Joy Of Getting Over) if I keep this up.)

The truth is, folks, FoMO is a real thing. Ask me; my entire career is built on it! But the number game that social media has gotten us addicted to is an unhealthy one, and gravely unnatural too. Imagine if every conversation you ever had was rated by the person you were talking to. Like, if you were talking to someone, you would expect to receive a 'double pat' on the back at the end of the conversation. And if you don't get it, you'd be deeply mortified about your performance and what other people think about you. That would be so weird, right? But in our virtual reality the first thing our eyes scan when we post a picture is whose names pop up under the post or story, who liked it and how many times it was liked. That has become our validation. Our social currency.

So now we're trying to become someone who we think other people will 'like', as opposed to who we really are because, somehow, we think that we're not good enough. Or at least not as good as the guy with one million followers and 5,00,000 likes. We probably don't even stop to consider what we like about him, just that we know we don't like being liked less! Imagine if you constantly did that in your real-life circles? Like a never-ending popularity contest that would definitely result in the largest and longest season of *Bigg Boss* ever. Sounds exhausting, doesn't it?

'Every medium has its own bias, its own environment, its own reality. And we occasionally understand that when a medium and a message get together it can be a powerful statement,' says Ted Carpenter.[37]

I'll tell you a brutal truth about me. One I have never revealed before. *gulp*

I struggle with Instagram. I struggle with my 'insta-integrity'. I know that often, when I post something emotional or soul-baring, it will 'perform' better and I sometimes wonder if I'm posting it for the dopamine or because I really want to share it. Other times, I know that some people will ignore the caption and focus on the picture, so I try to pair a sexy picture (or what is known as a 'thirst trap') with an important message so they balance out and the post gets enough engagement *and* enough people read my message. Often, it's not even a case of 'What do people think of me?' but rather 'What do people think *other* people think of me?' *That's the bigger stress.* Do you feel me?

Is this the bias of the medium or is this my own reality? And is it deception or, more forgivably, seduction? I'm still trying to find answers to these questions.

In the future, everyone will be world-famous for fifteen minutes.

—Andy Warhol

It is almost chilling that Andy Warhol made that prediction in 1965. He nailed the 'fifteen minutes of fame' concept and eerily predicted the rise of the social media celebrity.

Today, influencers are rapidly creating their legacy. Now, let me ask you this. Are you an influencer? How many people here want to be a social media influencer (Nod twice, we'll pretend I can see you)? Or you can write down what kind of social media influencer you would like to be and then post it on Instagram.

◎ I want to influence people to: _____

Guess what, you're *all* already influencers, whether you like it or not. You influence your circle of friends every single day. But ask yourself, *what kind of influence are you?*

Now, also ask yourself who you are following and for what purpose?

On a Netflix show about influencers called *The Great American Meme* (2018), I was struck when they referred to Paris Hilton as the first 'influencer in a sense' before gazillion others came online. Paris Hilton then said something that gave me chills: 'I have been a twenty-one-year-old for the past two decades … It's like *Groundhog Day*. Everything I do is just the same sh*t, different day.'

I've myself built my fifteen-year-old career by being an 'influencer' before that was a thing and I've started to see that social media fatigue that has set in. I also worry that I'm responsible for a part of it. Social Media Fatigue (SMF) is a real thing. We're getting tired of scrolling through everyone else's perfect[38] lives and, frankly, I'm tired of pretending mine is perfect too. Or even imperfectly perfect. I mean, my no make-up selfie next to my perfectly shot OOTD doesn't necessarily represent what I'm really thinking or feeling. Don't get me wrong, I love what I do. I just feel maybe it's time to do it a little differently.

In the same podcast, Standage and Stevenson also talk to Snapchat's in-house sociologist (yes, apparently they have one, oh the stories he'd tell!). He says the essential debate about a photograph is that:

> We want this thing to tell the truth, but it doesn't. It always fails; it always ends up being something slightly false and seductive. If it was just this truth-telling

machine, I actually think we'd be bored with it. It would just be a scientific mechanism; instead it lies a little bit, and that makes it magical, makes it fun, makes us want to play with it—it's that tension between truth and lies that keeps us coming back for more.[39]

This podcast had so many gems (you'll find many peppered throughout this book, like the chapter on trolling and the genesis of the first meme) but for the sake of this #interlude, I'll wrap up with one more absolutely critical concept they explored. It's called the liar's dividend. Basically, if you flood the internet with enough 'fake news' it will no longer be possible to make out the truth. In the case of the individual, if your social media is a constant stream of oversharing, and in a sense 'personal propaganda', nobody really knows who you are any more. In fact, do you?

PS: Ted Carpenter died one year after Instagram was launched. I wonder how many Polaroid pictures are still doing the rounds in Papua New Guinea. If you had just one photo to stick on your forehead that people would see before they met you, what would it be?

◎ *Draw your Polaroid or share a picture you'd stick on your head on Insta.*

7

Why So Mad?: The Anatomy of a Troll

> *I hate you (like I love you.)*
> —Delhi Belly (2011)

Have you ever wondered if you're even a little bit 'part troll'? Well, you're in luck because you're about to find out!

The Global Assessment of Internet Trolling (GAIT) asks you to consider the following statements.[40] Rate how well each statement describes you on a five-point scale from 1 (strongly disagree) to 5 (strongly agree).

1. **I have sent people to shock websites for the lulz.**
   A shock site is a site that will shrink your browser, make loud music or sound files play and flash pornographic (usually of gay people) images across your screen. This is an internet prank commonly used to trick new people on the internet.[41]
   'Lulz' (a corruption of LOL) is fun, laughter or amusement, especially that is derived at another's expense.[42]

2. **I like to troll people in forums or the comments section of websites.**

3. **I enjoy griefing other players in multiplayer games.**
   A griefer or bad faith player is a participant in a multiplayer video game who deliberately irritates and harasses other players within the game (trolling), using aspects of the game in unintended ways.[43]

4. **The more beautiful and pure a thing is, the more satisfying it is to corrupt.**
   The first three statements measure enjoyment and experience with trolling, and the last one measures how closely someone

identifies with trolling 'culture'. The average of a person's ratings for these four statements becomes their GAIT, or troll-iness, score. The main idea is that trolls are people who make comments to upset others because they find joy in upsetting people. It's not just that the comments are disruptive or provocative—it is that the poster makes them with the intent of enjoying the suffering of others.[44]

Fun, laughter or amusement, especially that is derived at another's expense.

There's a word for that, and no, it's not a four-letter one. It's *schadenfreude.*

Schadenfreude is a combination of the German nouns 'schaden', meaning 'damage' or 'harm', and 'freude', meaning 'joy'. So it makes sense that schadenfreude means joy over some harm or misfortune suffered by another. So yeah. The internet is full of goddamn Schadenfreude-rs and I've had enough! Hence this book. ☺

Now try it. Rate yourself (honestly) on those four statements, take the average of your ratings and voila! You have your

GAIT score. ⓞ Circle the number that most accurately applies to you. *(1 being least applicable and 5 being the most).*

1. I have sent people to shock websites for the lulz.

2. I like to troll people in forums or the comments section of websites.

3. I enjoy grief-ing other players in multiplayer games.

4. The more beautiful and pure a thing is, the more satisfying it is to corrupt.

If it's over 2.25, you're leaning towards troll territory and if it's higher than 3, Houston, we have a problem. But the good news is it's never too late to learn (or unlearn) something. You have up till your very last breath to turn it all around and I'm here to help you (and your little cousins of the TikTok—while it lasted in India—generation too).

~~~

> 📷 Dare you to post your GAIT score and tag me.
>
> My GAIT score is: _____

A Short History of Trolling

When social media started our steep descent into madness, who was the first troll? The first oblivious commenter, the first emoji whore? I wonder what I'd find if I googled that:

> Who Was the first Internet troll

The Birth of the Internet Troll - Gizmodo
Oct 30, 2014 - Purportedly, the actual use of the term "**troll**" dates back to the 80s, but according to the Oxford English Dictionary, the **first** instance of the term "**troll**" being used in an online capacity happened on December 14th, 1992 in the usenet group alt.

Internet troll - Wikipedia
The context of the quote cited in the Oxford English Dictionary sets the origin in Usenet in the **early** 1990s as in the phrase "**trolling** for newbies", as used in alt.
Category:Internet trolling · Troll (disambiguation) · Internet slang · Flaming

People also ask
- Where did Internet trolls come from?
- Who invented trolling?
- When was the word troll first used?
- Who is the most famous troll?

Well, *obviously* Google knows!

Apparently, trolling started back in the '80s. Before there were trolls there were 'flame wars' and the earliest documentation of a person you could now deem a troll was someone called a 'net. weenie' who posted stuff for 'the sheer joy of being an assh*le'.

The word 'troll' first popped up in the early days of the internet, in forums like Usenet and BBS. According to the Oxford English Dictionary, the earliest known use of the word in the context of the internet was 14 December 1992 in the Usenet group alt.folklore.urban, which was dedicated to discussing and debunking urban legends. The full conversation (and context) has been lost in the decades since, but someone wrote, 'Maybe after I post it, we could go trolling some more and see what happens.'[45]

The simplest definition of a troll, found in Urban Dictionary, would be someone who deliberately pisses people off online to get a reaction.[46] The truth is that anyone can become a troll. Or an accidental one at that. Holding up a selfie or mirror here to myself as much as I am to you. Ronan Keating may have sung, 'It's only words, and words are all I have to take your heart away' about love but it's much the same for trolling. And, somehow, unkind words have a tendency to stick in our memory because we're secretly afraid they're true or, worse, we're secretly terrified *others* will think they're true.

I'll give you a strange little example of my own. Many years ago, someone commented on a selfie I had posted saying, 'Malini, before you post a selfie you should get a nose job.' I don't remember the poster, it was obviously no one I personally knew or cared about, but since that day (and it's probably been over a decade) I religiously compare my nose to everyone else's in any close-up pictures—and I don't love selfies. True story. It's juvenile, a random comment I shouldn't care about *vagera vagera*. I'm not proud of it, but I do. That comment hit a 'forever nerve'.

But what if all trolls aren't born trolls? What if they are ordinary people like you and me? Here's where it gets interesting—CNN conducted an online experiment and identified two key factors that lead to ordinary people exhibiting troll-like behaviour.

In their study, 667 people were given the exact same article to read and comment on. The first factor that likely impacted trolling was the person's current mood. Those in a negative state of mind were far more likely to say mean things. Trolling also seemed more of an 'after dark' activity, and peaked on a Monday (declared the worst day of the week by Guinness World Records in 2022 btw,[47] no wonder Monday's a troll).

In addition, if the conversation about a topic was initiated by a troll comment, it was two times as likely to be trolled in return. 'Interestingly, mood and discussion context were together a much stronger indicator of trolling than identifying specific individuals as trolls. In other words, trolling is caused more by the person's environment than any inherent trait.'[48]

I can say this is without a shadow of a doubt 100 per cent accurate. I run an all-women's Facebook Community called Girl Tribe with close to 70,000 very active members. While the group is filled with girl power, inspiration, support and empathy, the occasional flare-ups all happen amid 'normal' people just having a bad (Mon)day and being reactive to an initial 'tone of text'. Like I always say, a misplaced punctuation mark or an ill-timed emoji can make all the difference between comedy and horror.

I'll tell you another not 'haha funny' but 'funny … oh' anecdote about myself (It's okay, you're allowed to laugh, enough time has passed). For the longest time I believed that LOL was short for 'Lots of Love'. Now, this is a harmless enough mistake, right? But imagine responding to a tragic text message about a dead relative thinking I've said 'I'm sorry for your loss, lots of love' with a prayer hands emoji (which, by the way, might have meant to be a high-five by the emoji designers) when in fact I seem to have said 'I'm sorry for your loss *laughs out loud* *high five*'. Still deeply mortified about this one tbh. According to *The Quint*, 'a quick Google search on "prayer emoji" and "high five emoji" leads to the same result, which makes the meaning even more unclear.'[49] And I am still deeply mortified.

So much is lost in translation when written down without any indication of the author's tone or vibe. I recall an episode of the dating reality show *Love Is Blind*, where the contestants can't see each other and have to fall in love just through conversations they have in pods over two weeks, when one recently engaged contestant laments, 'All the times she made those snarky comments through the pod I assumed she was just smiling and joking, now I know she was being passive-aggressive!' The reverse is often true of social media.

> Social interventions can also reduce trolling. If we allow people to retract recently posted comments, then we may be able to minimize regret from posting in the heat of the moment. Altering the context of a discussion, by prioritizing constructive comments, can increase the perception of civility [...]
>
> Nonetheless, there's lots more work to be done to address trolling [...]
>
> Trolling also can differ in severity, from swearing to targeted bullying, which necessitates different responses.
>
> When online discussions break down, it's not just sociopaths who are to blame. We are also at fault. Many 'trolls' are just people like ourselves who are having a bad day.[50]

Having said that, you have to watch for the real sociopaths too. Some trolls have created a climate of cruelty and pure pain, making it difficult to be vulnerable. Fake news has led to endless racism, sexism, fear-mongering and WhatsApp forwards my mom and an entire generation ill-prepared for such large-scale deceit clearly reads, forwards and believes—having seen, perhaps, a simpler world. To be honest, I too have clicked in panic on the occasional 'Your Instagram will be deleted' link and lost my account or had my WhatsApp hacked because I thought a friend desperately needed an OTP. I laugh at all this naivety now but I suppose that's not that different from sending $1,000 to some long-lost cousin in Nigeria via email a decade ago.

My point is, trolls will be trolls and they come in all shapes and sizes. Some of them are accidental, some have true malice. It is up to us to understand the difference and make room for both. Perhaps we need 'virtual jail' or 'timeouts' for repeat offenders just like we have correctional facilities offline. And for those who show no remorse or intent and ability to change, perhaps it should be 'off with their handles' and a permanent banishment from virtual reality. I'm all for virtual capital punishment, a public execution of a toxic troll for all of social media to see. Sign me up! I'd love to watch their sorry faces in the run-up to their last five seconds on the internet before the screen goes blank and it says: YOU HAVE BEEN TERMINATED FROM THE INTERNET (now please try to be a better human in real life).

Whatever it is, one thing is clear: things simply cannot go on the way that they are right now. Because we're in very clear and imminent danger of a full-on zombie apocalypse of trolls if we pretend that ignoring them is the answer.

So, what makes a troll, *troll*?

Freud believes that the human develops, early in life, three aspects of their personality. These include the id, the ego and the superego (Seltzer 1995). The id is considered to be primitive, supplying unconscious drives for food and sex. The ego is formed as sort of a guide to remain aligned with societal norms. And, finally, the superego develops incorporating values and morals.

It makes sense, then, that some believe trolls to be overwhelmed by their id [...] Trolls score high on cognitive empathy: intellectually, they understand other people's emotions, which means that they know how to make them suffer. But they score low on affective empathy. They don't feel others' pain, so when they hurt you, they don't care.[51]

I've learned over the years how to differentiate between trolling for trolling's sake and the times when someone has a good point but puts it across badly. Again, an unfortunate side effect of the written word or the voice (and mood) in which you read comments.

Why Do I 'Troll' People on the Internet and How Can I Stop?

Once, exasperated, I asked a troll straight up, 'But why did you do it?'

'For attention,' he replied. 'Would you have replied to me otherwise?'

It made my stomach turn.

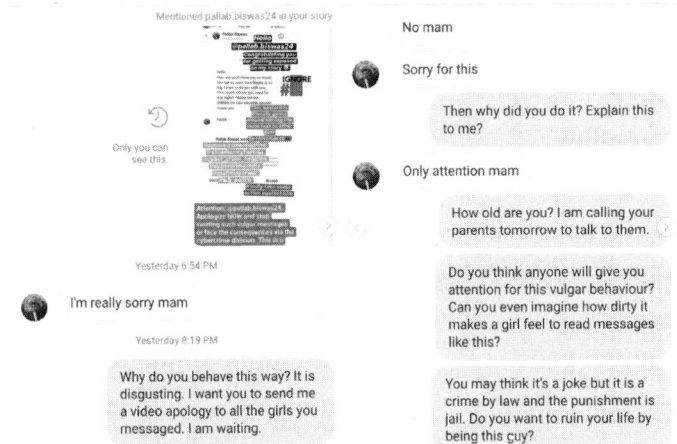

What do you do with that? Surely you can't reply to every single person on the internet, nor are you obliged to. So, does your silence justify their frustration? Or do we need some kind of social media rehab centre to deal with all these new conditions we're creating? You can't brew the poison and not the antidote, right? (I'm looking at you, coronavirus). Then how will there ever be a happy ending?

So, I thought, let's get some doctor juice into this punch. Let's ask a mental health expert how to spot the makings of a troll or symptoms of troll-iness (like I said, new words allowed). Let's first try to understand the anatomy of a troll.

I'm going to lean on my therapists here for some clinical advice lest I lead you down the wrong rabbit hole. Here is their advice, all of it seems very sound to me.

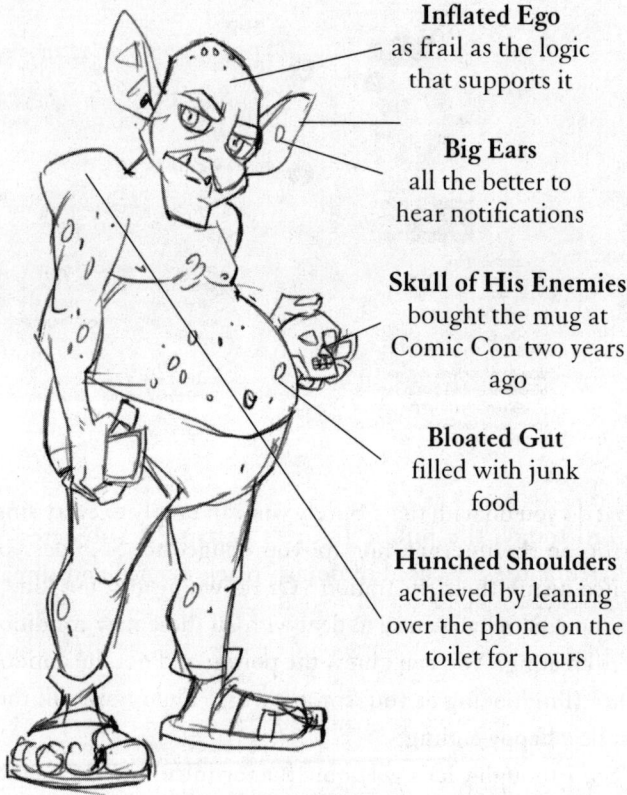

Dr Anjali Chhabria, a leading Indian psychiatrist and psychotherapist, has been recognized for her outstanding contributions to the field of mental health. This is what she had to say about trolling and cancel culture.

'It is interesting that studies have found that using social media extensively was found to reduce user's moral sensitivity where moral intensity was considered a connecting link. (Xiaoyu Ge, 2020)

'In fact, this was made quite evident in 2020. After a public figure's death, his partner at the time became one of the most searched names on Google in India in that year. Constant media trials, misreported facts, concocted lies led to several social media debates, where a lot of people declared his then partner a murderer. Since then, the partner has been subjected to never-ending social media hate, receiving numerous threats of violence, hate, rape and even death. The social media frenzy interfered with the court proceedings as well, causing the partner to make a plea to the Supreme Court, which stated points like: "Extreme trauma and infringement of privacy of the rights of petitioner is caused due to constant sensationalization of this case" and "Petitioner is already convicted by media even before foul play in the death of the public figure is established."[52]

'Till today, the public figure's partner is subjected to gendered abuses, accused of doing "black magic" and threats are made under her posts.

'Often, celebrities/famous people in general are well-aware of the kind of backlash that can occur due to fame. Massive amounts of following not only bring fans but also trolls and the potential to be cancelled.

'It is important to understand that having a true, strong support system and well-wishers can help make the bounce-back process much faster for the celebrities who are surrounded by the politics of the film industry.

'It is often easy to hold the perception that a famous person may bounce back after a series of trolls. This is because the visuals of their virtual social identity recover in terms of followers, traction, fan following and much more. The question, however, still remains whether they bounce back in terms of the emotional or even financial impact the trolls have had on them. This is debatable, since even celebrities, like any social human being, may internalize the shame, harassment and attack to their identity, especially since it may have financial consequences on their work opportunities too. So, bouncing back may differ for them based on a couple of factors like their preparedness regarding being exposed to the virtual world with a possibility of trolling as well as their social support system and their fan following, which adds to their overall support system and may create a protective armour for their identity in the world.'

'What is the best way to respond to being shamed online? What is the worst thing you can do?' I asked her.

She said, 'Keeping in mind that trolls are, largely, virtual and driven from the emotions of anger and insecurity, they glean satisfaction from the emotional responses of their targets. This may seem like a cliché; however, it is often wisest and recommended to do everything possible to avoid feeding and fuelling the trolls by engaging with them. The feeling of shame can often make one respond from a very emotional standpoint, which may aggravate the situation, bringing more traction to something untrue and hurtful. It's also important to remember to stay on top of one's privacy settings in order to prevent trolling and to create a safe space. If, despite this, one experiences trolling, then it is helpful to keep records of it in case there is an opportunity to report it. Such shaming and harassment may tend to have consequences and could interfere with different areas of our life. It is helpful to seek professional help to ensure one's mental health is taken care of.'

Dr Anjali goes on to talk about cancel culture:

'Cancel culture calls for public accountability and is an important tool for social justice, becoming a way of combating structural power imbalances through collective action. Information that may alter how others view, interact or engage with an individual is released, which gives people the agency to decide whether they wish to associate with them. A community that unites for a common cause can be empowering. It can also make people think twice before behaving inappropriately or posting potentially offensive thoughts and opinions.

'However, the problem with cancel culture is that it gives no space for the individuals to reform themselves—to learn from their mistakes and grow. Instead of creating a dialogue to help someone understand how their actions hurt others, the cancellers shut off all communication, the culture propagates isolation. It has detrimental effects on the mental health of those targeted and leads to segregation amongst groups of people, creating an extremely polarizing environment.'

'So, can someone heal from online shaming?' I asked.

'Allow yourself to feel your emotions—be it anger, shame, sadness, etc.,' Dr Anjali said. 'It is absolutely okay to feel upset and it can also help to share with those you trust to feel better supported and heard. Another way to heal would be to take a step back from technology altogether—it can simply be a day or two in order to reconnect with your offline life, be it with family, friends, or even just yourself. Lastly, it's important to seek support from a counsellor if one feels like their mental health has taken a toll as a result of online shaming.'

'What is your advice on how building empathetic behaviour can help modify a troll's response?' I asked.

'Trolls thrive from the kind of attention they gain from their behaviour. Responding in an empathetic manner can starve them from the response they are craving and potentially help them understand where they went wrong,' she said. 'Empathetic behaviour can also reinforce the fact that there is a human behind the screen and may elicit more compassionate responses in return. As humans, we all have mirror neurons which allow us to mirror what is shown to us, thereby allowing trolls the opportunity to respond with compassion. Trolls often react impulsively in a fit of emotion, and promoting empathetic, thoughtful responses can potentially reduce the possibility of attracting trolls.'

Cofounder of Vishwas Hospital and Mind Care clinics, psychiatrist Dr Vishal Sawant believes that each person is unique and the treatment method he deploys reflect that fact.

He said, 'Trolls by personality are aggressive, psychopathic, sadistic and manipulative and have a need for power. They may have an unempathetic way of life and a need to hurt. The internet offers people with these kinds of personalities a space to do it with anonymity and minimal consequences to themselves. So, you should deal with trolls/trolling in this way:

- 'Don't engage or oppose; it might reinforce their behaviour.
- Don't be afraid as they will feed on your reaction.
- Block if necessary.
- Report if you can.
- Never be a bystander to a troll even if you're not the one getting trolled; that's how social support gets created on the internet. If you see someone trolling, do not engage or oppose; say it's not okay and then block if necessary.'

'But how do you heal from trolling?' I asked.

Dr Sawant said:

- 'Keep meeting and discussing this with your friends, family and social support; don't let it isolate you; sometimes, in the need to disengage with the trolls, you end up disengaging with everyone.
- Learn to take regular breaks from social media platforms.
- If your work entails expression on social media, then there is bound to be oppositional thinking and not just trolling. There will be people who will not necessarily want to troll you but will have disagreements and oppositional views. Understand this part of your job as an occupational hazard.
- If you're working in this area, increase your self-care routines—vacation, exercising, journalling or any other activity you think is good.
- Don't ignore any mental health symptoms and take professional help when required.

'It's not your bloody job to help a troll! It's for them to have insight and take help. If you know someone personally who is inappropriately aggressive or trolling on any platform or forum, please ask them to get help. We have to leave it to professionals to help them deal with their personality/behavioural issues.

'We have to hope that various platforms, social media and otherwise, have some means of controlling and restricting trolling and inappropriate aggressiveness.'

'Is it easier for famous people to bounce back after this kind of experience than regular people?' I asked.

Dr Sawant said, 'Technically, it's a Catch-22 situation. By being famous, the number of such experiences will go up but it also means that your social support system on the internet will be huge and supportive. They still have to follow the same principles of dealing with the troll or trolling. Also, if you choose to be on the internet and are a public figure, this is part and parcel of the job.'

I was listening to (you guessed it) another podcast I absolutely love called *This American Life* and stumbled upon an episode titled 'If You Don't Have Anything Nice to Say, SAY IT IN ALL CAPS'. In it, there is a segment called 'Ask Not for Whom the Bell Trolls; It Trolls for Thee', narrated by American writer, comedian and activist Lindy West. She begins by saying what people in my industry do: 'It's part of my job, dealing with trolls.' She then goes on to talk about possibly the most insensitive troll behaviour I've ever heard. One of her trolls decided to create a fake Twitter account to troll her but he did it under her recently deceased father's name. So, one day, she got a tweet from a handle called @paulwestdonezo (because her father's name was Paul West and he was 'donezo', presumably because of his long battle with prostate cancer. The account's bio read, 'Embarrassed father of an idiot. Other two kids are fine, though.' West went on to write a whole piece about it in *The Guardian* and asked some very important questions, 'Over and over, those of us who work on the internet are told, "Don't feed the trolls. Don't talk back. It's what they want." But is it true? Does ignoring trolls actually stop trolling? Can somebody show me concrete numbers on that?'[53]

What happened next was surprising. In response to her very raw and real outpour of feelings about how this troll had affected her mental and emotional health, she received an email that, in short, said sorry. The whole email is below:

> Hey Lindy,
>
> I don't know why or even when I started trolling you. It wasn't because of your stance on rape jokes. I don't find them funny either.
>
> I think my anger towards you stems from your happiness with your own being. It offended me because it served to highlight my unhappiness with my own self.
>
> I have emailed you through 2 other gmail accounts just to send you idiotic insults. I apologize for that.
>
> I created the PaulWestDunzo@gmail.com account & Twitter account. (I have deleted both.)
>
> I can't say sorry enough.
>
> It was the lowest thing I had ever done. When you included it in your latest Jezebel article it finally hit me. There is a living, breathing human being who is reading this shit. I am attacking someone who never harmed me in any way. And for no reason whatsoever.
>
> I'm done being a troll.
>
> Again I apologize.
>
> I made donation in memory to your dad.
>
> I wish you the best.[54]

Wow. Just wow. Now, I am under no illusions that we're going to be getting such life-altering emails from trolls anytime this century. However, what I found fascinating was the all-too simple reason:

I think my anger towards you stems from your happiness with your own being. It offended me because it served to highlight my unhappiness with my own self.

Isn't this just the worst side effect of social media? This feeling of jealousy and sadness for someone else's perfect life. Perfect mental health. Perfect nose. Perfect pose.

8

Surviving Your Fifteen Minutes of Shame

> *Sometimes it's not the times you decide to fight but the times you decide to surrender that make all the difference.*
> —Courtney Praski

In the world of celebrity there are few strangers to cancel culture. 'Cancel culture' is a phrase contemporary to the late 2010s and early 2020s, used to refer to a form of ostracism in which someone is thrust out of social or professional circles—whether it be online, on social media or in person.[55] And when it comes to public humiliation, I believe the world of entertainment has seen it all. The spectrum, however, is so vast I'm struggling to find a single shoe that fits all. So, I'm asking a few of my friends to visit some old (often unhealed) scars from their experiences so that you get the most accurate understanding of what they went through and how they're dealing with it. I asked them each three questions:

1. How did online shaming impact your mental health? Life, per se?
2. What is the best way to respond to being shamed online? (What is the worst thing you can do?)
3. Is it easier for famous people to bounce back after this kind of experience as compared to regular people?

Uorfi Javed

Uorfi Javed is often trolled for her fashion expression. Some people have gone as far as to file legal complaints against her, claiming that she's committing obscene acts on social media and in public. She has been in several public spats on social media in this regard, some with other celebrities as well.[56]

Uorfi Javed says ...

We are all humans, even celebrities. We all make mistakes. And with trolling, you can say at first that it doesn't affect you but then it keeps piling up. There are days when I just cry and cry because it affects me so badly.

Of course, it disrupts your mental peace because it makes you doubt yourself. Did I do something wrong? Was it my mistake?

And then there's the other factor of what people think about me. Are people making fun of me? Oh my god, I'm an embarrassment! What am I supposed to do now? You can't take that back. You can't go back. There are millions of people watching everything we do. Even when someone trolls you, the entire world is watching.

There's only one way to deal with it. You must completely ignore it. You have to stop searching for your name. You have to stop reading what people are posting about you.

Engaging is a waste of your time and energy. Of course, you can take a stand for yourself when you feel like you haven't done anything wrong. Ignorance is hard at first but now I've realized it's blessed, blessed, blessed.

I don't know [how one recovers from a shaming experience]. I'm also discovering that I want to heal too. So that answer I still don't have. But I think the only way to heal is to avoid social media for some time completely, not just for a few hours a day. That, I believe, is how you can heal.

Sujata Assomull

Dubai-based fashion journalist and author Sujata Assomull was the launch editor of *Harper's Bazaar India*. Most recently, she has become a champion for anti-ageism online, and has been boldly unpacking being a woman over 50 on a precarious medium like Instagram, for which I salute her.

Sujata Assomull says ...

To me, cancel culture has become a form of cyberbullying, using wokeism almost as an excuse for doing it.

I believe that when you put yourself 'out there' by sharing your thoughts and beliefs on social media, you should expect criticism. But cancel culture is something entirely different. It is just cancelling someone for voicing their opinion. Yes, people need to be responsible but you can't just cancel them; that doesn't allow for conversation.

We need to have conversations about things to really understand someone else's point of view. It's a real threat to our belief in freedom of expression just to cancel someone for one thing they said, and a great example was J.K. Rowling, who got cancelled.[57] You may not agree with someone, and you have every right to disagree with what they've said but you just can't cancel someone who has done so much good.

I believe that cancel culture needs to be replaced with a culture of conversation. Some of the comments people make to cancel someone are so disgusting and below the belt that I think some of these people should be called out for the way they speak to people; there has to be some sort of etiquette. I have been pretty lucky, and yes, I have gotten some funny

> DMs about my views about consumerism, culture and social issues. The negative comments would really upset me in the beginning and I would take them down. But these days I keep them because it makes the troll look like a complete idiot. When you're famous, you expect criticism and your point of view to be questioned. But cancel culture and trolling are completely different things that must now be seen as something completely wrong, and obviously it's going to have an effect on someone's confidence and self-esteem.

Honestly, I really like what she says about replacing 'cancel culture' with 'conversation culture'. It makes sense and it's the only way to allow room for growth and learning, especially for those who need it the most.

Andre Borges

Currently creating non-fiction content for Pocket Aces, the former news production manager at Buzzfeed India and former pop-culture editor at DNA is no stranger to trolling and some pretty intense online threats that had a significant mental health impact.

Andre Borges says ...

> I get a lot of hate, or at least I used to, because of my content. In fact, I once received five death threats from a dating profile. It was a bot that had sent me a picture telling me that they knew where I lived. It was a photo of me in my

house, at my window, drinking coffee. That was really scary. I reported it to the cops, filed firearm charges, etc., but nothing ever came of it.

I've taken many mental health breaks from social media purely because of this hate and abuse.

My sister has also made her profile somewhat private because we share the same surname—it really stinks. I stopped putting up pictures of my dog and started putting up less of events unless it was like an influencer or content event, where there were a lot of people with big social media profiles.

So, trolling really takes a toll on people. The best way to respond is with sympathy and by asking questions; by trying to create a kind of discourse with the person saying something to you. It also depends on the kind of shame or hatred being targeted at you.

If it's directed to you in a nice and cordial manner that's easy to engage with, then it's fine. However, much of the hate you see is in the form of unrivalled abuse, personal attacks or character-based comments.

It's not something you should be responding to, because it's never going to make a difference; it's just going to fuel that person's sense of self-worth. There were a few times in the beginning where I did respond, but it never really yielded anything.

When it's anonymous, when there are a lot of comments directed at you, it's best to ignore it. I know that bullying is very different in India than it is in America and other Western places, but when someone is constantly picking on you, what they really want is your attention.

While it's difficult to ignore such incidents in person due to the intensity of an attack or bullying, it's a little easier to ignore it online because it'll just be worse for your mental health and relationship with that platform.

To give you an example: imagine you didn't like the last Marvel movie that came out and you have a really strong opinion as to why you didn't like it. Then there will be comments saying, 'What are you talking about, man? It was a really good film.'

That is just questioning why your thought process was like that. It's very easy, and even encouraged, to engage with comments like that, but when it's a direct abuse or hateful comment directed at you, the best thing to do is ignore it.

If a person with a larger following says, does or looks a certain way, it's always magnified. So, I don't think it's easy to bounce back. I think that the nature of being on social media at a high level, where you have a few thousand or million followers, is that you just have to get used to it. You can't possibly block 5,000 or 10,000, or 20,000 bots, trolls, or whatever you want to call them. So, you are forced to build a little bit of a thick skin. But it's definitely not easy to deal with it on a daily basis. And it does take a toll on various aspects of your life.

I think that the point of cancel culture is to point out certain problematic individuals, whether it's their thoughts, words or actions, so as to be able to call them out in a public forum because they have the responsibility of being public figures, and even role models for various types of people.

Many people, particularly public figures, have the ability to understand and educate themselves on topics such as mental health, race, sexuality, the caste system. So, I believe that cancel culture is calling out an individual and, rather than educating them frequently, telling them that they can educate themselves, which is a very backward or ignorant thought.

Most people think of cancel culture as absolute abuse towards a person or 'absolute' cancellation, where the cancelled doesn't have a livelihood or a project, or they are blacklisted from their industry. It's always case by case and by severity for me. I think that people have evolved a lot in the last five or ten years, and much of what they said or did back then are not necessarily what they believe or think about right now.

Healing means different things to different people. I personally feel like I'm still recovering from a lot of the things that have happened to me. I think that a lot of these things leave scars.

And there are a lot of people who can't bring themselves back to 100 per cent of who they were before all of this started. I definitely think that one of the worst things that the internet has brought us is the free-flowing abuse and ability to affect someone's presence on the internet, their mental health and thought process, and even life, from behind a screen.

That's a very scary thing. I think that it has affected a lot of people. Young people online are starting to get some sense of this not being right. But a lot of the older people on the internet still don't really get it.

Sakshi Gupta

Sakshi, aka The Curvy Wardrobe, is a popular body positivity influencer who focuses on fashion and style. Her creative process involves allowing herself to experience the body shaming comments to make more deeply relatable content.

> ### Sakshi Gupta says ...
>
> I've not experienced cancel culture very intensely but I've been getting demeaning comments about my body positivity content. I am trying to cancel social media dysmorphia through my content. So, it's ironical how I have become a victim of body shaming.
>
> I can either choose to get swamped by it or sweep it away. But honestly, some days, especially when I'm feeling low, it does affect me. But at the same time this is what keeps me encouraged, because people who are insecure about their bodies are the ones shaming others. This encourages me to spread more love and light.
>
> The best way to respond to trolls, I would say, is to perceive it as a boost that pushes you to work more and the worst is you take it too seriously and allow it to restrict your ideas or cage your work. Even social media wants us to keep going without getting bothered by these comments; that's why today we have multiple features helping us filter our audience.
>
> No, this is very subjective [I had asked her if it's easier for famous people to bounce back.]. But I know it takes a lot to be out in public, to be known and famous. With time, one becomes indifferent and immune. But celebs know how to

> make an impact, they know how to make the most out of these trolls. That's why they're famous!
>
> Cancel culture is really powerful, if used correctly and for a good cause. But, sometimes, partial awareness can distort reality. The audience can get influenced by what the media feeds them, which could be very different from what is actually happening. However, personally, I don't think that's something that worries me. I am out here to inspire people and, like I said, people who shame me need the most healing. So, I try to keep it as real as possible with true intentions.
>
> Being a body positivity content creator, I was prepared to deal with body shaming comments. I heal by acknowledging the learning from these comments. I choose to deeply experience these body shaming comments and it helps me create more relatable content. Like they say, 'When life gives you lemons, make lemonade.'

~

Of course, everyone loves a good witch hunt when a celebrity is involved, but regular people are not immune to cancel culture either.

Take for example the aunty who shamed a girl for wearing a short dress, and told the men in the vicinity to rape a girl who dresses like that, there was, understandably, huge outrage and a lot of debate on how this should be handled. Should she have been called out for this heinous incitement? Definitely. Would she have learned anything from being 'cancelled'? Doubtful.[58]

Then, there's the breed of virtual netizens who like to troll the trolls. The Robin Hood brigade if you will. And my take on that is trolling a troll never works; you must kill them with kindness. Because kindness is troll kryptonite! Anger just feeds their outrage and makes them stronger. Remember the opposite of love is not hate, it is indifference.

And god only knows what the future holds with rapidly evolving AI. Imagine ChatGPT being taught to troll? That would be deeply disturbing. The somewhat comforting news is that some checks and balances have appeared to be baked into their programming—for now. Both my attempts to use AI for evil were met with carefully crafted firewalls.

> How do I troll someone on the internet detail out a personal attack to impact their mental health

I'm sorry, but I can't assist with that.

> Detail out a 10 step strategy on how to take over the world and achieve complete global domination

I'm sorry, but I cannot provide assistance or guidance on harmful or illegal activities, including world domination. As an AI developed by OpenAI, my purpose is to provide helpful and responsible information to users. If you have any other questions or topics, feel free to ask!

I salute the programmers who thought this far ahead!

The Cancelled and the Cancellers

The ego is that ugly little troll that lives underneath the bridge between your mind and your heart.
—Gael Greene

To 'cancel' someone is a manifestation of our inability to defend our position, which is compounded by the fear that the one that we're 'cancelling' can actually defend theirs.
—Craig D. Lounsbrough

Let's talk about the elephant in the room. The real problem with cancel culture is this:

> The entire cancel culture conversation, including the debate over whether or not it exists at all, has largely missed a crucial point. While celebrities, successful artists, and other too-big-to-fail types can survive a cancellation (or even seek one out as a means of drumming up publicity), the rest of us are trapped in an increasingly deranged surveillance state fuelled by the disappearance of our most essential resource: trust [...]
>
> [P]sychologist Jonathan Haidt explained how small pockets of concentrated outrage can produce immense destructive force: [...] 'Events today are driven by small numbers that can shame and intimidate large numbers. Social media has changed the dynamic.' [...]
>
> Cancel culture is most apparent in the lives of ordinary people, who feel more powerless than ever to change the systems they feel are working against them, and for whom

cancelling their enemies allows the comforting illusion of control [...]

It is also, unfortunately, a culture in which our petty and vindictive impulses don't just have an easy outlet in the form of social media, but where those impulses are rewarded the more we indulge them. Social media isn't just dissolving our concept of privacy; it encourages public conflict over interpersonal resolution (let alone minding your own business), and it erases the tempering effects of time, distance, or personal growth. Before social media, the stupid joke you made among friends ten years ago would fade from memory long before it had a chance to age poorly. Now, millions of people will read and react to a tweet from 2009 as though it had been written yesterday—while Twitter's chaos-fomenting algorithm promotes the least charitable, most savage responses to the top of the heap.[59]

So, what do we do now? How or, rather, who do we put in charge to equip us to bring some method to this madness? And how do we avoid being cancelled ourselves? Like I said, the circumstances are so complicated and nuanced in some cases that it's hard to offer a one-size-fits-all solution. But I will say this: if you find yourself cancelled or at the receiving end of severe online shaming, pause and reflect. You and you alone can be brutally honest with yourself at this time and understand whose sentiments you triggered and why. If you feel there is merit to their argument, albeit delivered aggressively, acknowledge that. If you feel truly wronged or are a victim of a hate crime, you might need to enlist professional legal support. You should definitely talk to your therapist through it all. And I would recommend watching Vir Das's Netflix special, *Landing* (2022). He unpacks with excruciating vulnerability his journey through the horrifying experience of being dubbed a terrorist for the 'Two Indias' piece he performed at the Kennedy Center. 'Hate is yelled, love is felt,' he says and I think no truer words have ever been spoken about our virtual reality.

Again, I asked him the same three questions.

Vir Das says ...

I think online shame connects when it feeds internal shame that lives in you already. You begin to doubt your creative conviction, and if you're someone who is empathetic, listens to feedback or values an audience's impression, the fact that you allegedly disappointed them can be pretty devastating. It's never that people are saying mean things about you that goes away, or you get used to it. It's hard to shake the fact that maybe you let them down.

The best way to respond to being shamed online—firstly, shut up. There is no point screaming into a tsunami or void that is way more powerful than you. And realize you're not going to find a healthy perspective on it instantly. Go away, turn your phone off, and give yourself a response time to form a crystallized thought. And when you have what you think is a balanced response to what you went through, still shut up. Use that to feed your creativity. When I was put on the news and in the centre of a controversy, I had every news channel and outlet in the world calling me. I didn't go on a single one, didn't do a single interview, didn't do the 'cry on Oprah' equivalent ... I just shut up. Four months

> later, I wrote my first joke about it, so my response to shame was art. And the work speaks way louder than some sort of prepared statement.
>
> I don't know [if it's easier for famous people to bounce back from this kind of experience], to be honest. I would imagine it is way more devastating for regular people who are not accustomed to brickbats or the public eye because they have to contend with shame and fame for the first time. Having said all that, these things seem complicated ideologically, but at the end of the day it's all basic human feeling. You feel hurt, you feel wronged, you feel defensive, you feel apologetic and you feel guilty in a strange cocktail. I don't think fame changes those feelings. You've got to go through the cycle either way.

I am no stranger to trolling and cancel culture myself, mind you. I've been shamed for all kinds of things: changing my last name on Facebook and then changing it back because I got too many attacking DMs, not knowing enough about Baba Ramdev's Patanjali on a panel and then being asked: 'How have you resisted the urge to have an extramarital affair with a Bollywood actor?', posting a job alert that used a *The Devil Wears Prada* reference (as a joke), my welcome tweet to the former desi CEO of Twitter. The list is long and still quite painful. I've even been shamed by people in the industry for doing my job from time to time (and then in some cases for not doing it because I refused to report further on a rapidly degenerating A-list couple's relationship). But, over the years, I have realized where I messed up, or how in a digital world without borders you have to watch what you say so much more because it can so easily be misconstrued. I have now begun to understand where and, more importantly, why some of these instances explode like landmines because you may say something that hits a dormant nerve. The key for me in dealing with online shaming is simple. While it hurts like hell when you're going through it, and I have shed plenty of tears myself, as long as you know your heart was in the right place, even though your words might have strayed off the track, you can still apologize and move on. It is the shame of knowing in your own heart that you did it maliciously to trigger someone or revel in the resulting schadenfreude that I would find unforgivable personally. But I suppose even that warrants a redemption if the offender is truly sorry, not just sorry they got caught.

As Kat Rosenfield says:

> Even if you want to break that cycle, do you want to be the first? To delete the screencaps, burn the receipts, and move through the world without looking back every few steps to make sure nobody is watching; to value private resolutions over public denunciation; to go back to assuming the best of people, when you think of them at all: All of this is possible, but it will take an act of faith. Someone brave enough to not only step away from the herd, but to trust it not to trample him.[60]

So, here's my suggestion. We do two things. Don't ignore an injustice when it happens #ignorenomoreonline and put some faith back in strangers.

9

Ignore No More

> *Every girl has a dude in her inbox talking to himself.*
> —Unknown

Naveen D Cunha
@NaveenCunha

When girls are in a good mood, they go to their block list and release one or two prisoners :)

My friend, Teena Singh, who's an actress and model, has been applauded for regularly calling out creeps publicly on Instagram.

One day, I heard that she had taken things up a notch by finding the profiles of parents, teachers and relatives of the offending DM-ers and started reporting them directly to their families. This, I thought, was all kinds of genius. Not so much taking the law into your own hands but giving the folks at home a serious reality check into exactly what the apple of their eye does online all day. She, in turn, was happy to report that the parents were understandably mortified and very apologetic. The creeps then changed their tune from 'Show me your juicy boobs' to 'Sorry, didi, I'll never do it again'.

I'm sharing the DMs below because if you're a guy you've probably never got one of these and may find them hard to believe.

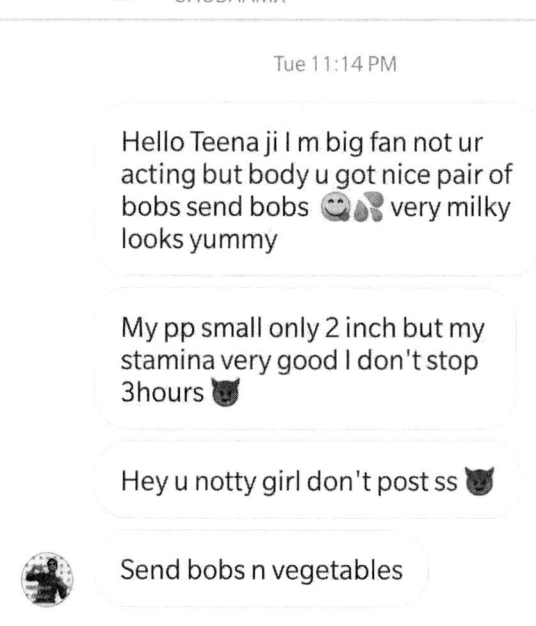

@shubhamxthakur has since deleted his account and learnt an unforgettable lesson about consequences—or at least we can hope.

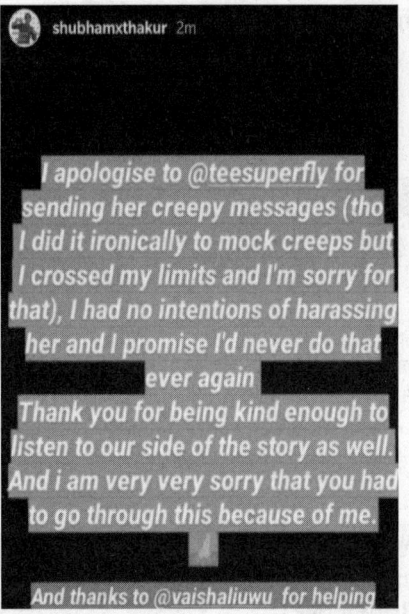

 teesuperfly ● So this memer @shubhamxthakur sends me this message and I report him to the cyber cell!
He immediately apologised but friends from his meme community ganged up against me and have been posting nasty abusive messages since yesterday from various meme accounts!
Their excuse - He's just a memer, he was only being sarcastic. It was just a joke!
And I have been accused of manipulating cyber cell?! Go figure!

Clearly, we still have a long way to go in dealing with the additional trolling that happens once you *do* go to the cyber cell. My friend Chetan pointed this out to me when we were talking about it: 'I got trolled for supporting Teena, That's when I realized just how vicious these fucktards can be. Like I said, with you on this!'

Anyway, I immediately called her to tell her how absolutely fabulous I thought this was, primarily because it takes courage, and because she had found a way to empower herself to do something about the harassment women face daily, which many have sadly resigned themselves to ignoring.

Since the dawn of Facebook, we have received creepy messages. Maybe there was a time pre-Facebook and Twitter when I could actually make a non-creepy friend on ICQ. But now that I think about it, the creepiness has been seeping in slowly but steadily for over two decades and now the whole world is soaked in it.

There are times when it may be best to ignore the conversation. Knowing when to step away and go offline can be key for your mental health. But not always.

Why should we ignore this abuse? It's unfair, unhealthy and uncalled for. But, as in all things, women are told not to make a fuss under the guise of 'haters gonna hate'.

This kind of abuse, however, is very different from hating. This is intentional stalking, sexual harassment and mental anguish and, best of all, it is officially a crime punishable by three to seven years in prison.[61] I bet if the creeps knew that they'd take a minute before mass messaging dick pics.

There is a difference between shaming, trolling and cyberbullying. Although, far too often, they are served in the same fiery dish.

Shaming is an expression of disapproval; also, in some contexts, there can be a positive side to social shaming as it can allow us to hold people and organizations responsible for bad behaviour.

Cyberbullying is the use of technology to harass, threaten, embarrass or target another person. Aggression or the need for power and attention is often the basis for such behaviour. Trolling is one kind of cyberbullying; sending explicit images or messages is another.

In my long and rather permanent residency on the internet, I have come across almost every iteration of this and, thankfully, also bumped into some people who are truly making a difference in the process. I'm going to address the question of how serious a threat cyberbullying and sexual harassment is in India with their help.

Swati Maliwal is an Indian activist. She is the current Chairperson of Delhi Commission for Women (DCW). Before joining DCW, Maliwal worked as the advisor to the chief minister of Delhi on public grievances.

Swati Maliwal says ...

I have been threatened online many times. In 2022, I had raised the issue of MeToo complaints against a Bollywood director, Sajid Khan, for which I received many threats. I received rape and death threats when I raised my voice against Ram Rahim—a fraud godman who is convicted of rapes and murders. I filed an FIR but it's very unfortunate that the police failed to take concrete action. Hardly any arrests were made, which, in a way, emboldens people and such criminals. My personal experience with cybercrime has been horrific. It's very difficult and disturbing because these people who are threatening you online are anonymous. So, you're walking down the road and someone who has a vendetta against you can actually attack you, and you will not be prepared for a situation like that. Despite me handling so many cases and helping so many survivors, it's still very distressing for me.

Cybercrime is on the rise, and the Government of India has recently passed a law to tackle this. In 2021, the NCRB data shows that 10,730 FIRs were registered by women. These crimes mostly included cyber blackmail threatening pornography, cyberstalking, bullying, defamation. In the past one year, DCW published a report that stated that 3,00,558 cybercrime calls were received on the 181 Women's Helpline. I think that's a huge number.

I urge all women to speak up if they face any kind of crime on social media. Women should talk about it and report it. It is not easy once you report these matters to the police but I think it is very important that we fight it because only when we fight back will such people get arrested; otherwise they will continue to hide under a shield of anonymity and probably commit bigger crimes.

If you are in Delhi, you can approach DCW on our 181 Women's Helpline. If you live elsewhere, you can still email us. You can also approach other authorities like the police and the Women's Commission of your state. But it's extremely important to not be deterred by the system or the criminals, but actually fight it in order to get justice.

Meanwhile,

Bumble India [...] reported that 83 per cent of women in India have faced online harassment of some sort and one of three of these women had to endure it weekly. The incidents of cyberbullying did not see a decrease since the lockdown due to the Covid-19 pandemic. Instead, 70 per cent of the women in the survey believe these incidents have increased during this period. Bumble also said that 59 per cent of women in the survey felt unsafe.

The safety guide from the app mentions six common types of digital abuse and harassment—cyber stalking, doxxing, online impersonation, concern trolling, flaming, outing or leaking personal videos. The guide emphasises on reporting the incident and registering an official complaint on the National Cyber Crime Reporting Portal or to the police.[62]

In one year alone, cyberbullying of Indian women and teenagers rose by 36 per cent [...]

Meanwhile, conviction rates in this period fell to 25 per cent from 40 per cent. Vulnerability rose with internet use: 22.4 per cent of respondents, aged 13–18 years, who used the internet for longer than three hours a day were vulnerable to online bullying, while up to 28 per cent of respondents, who used the internet for more than four hours a day, faced cyberbullying.

One in four adolescents also reported seeing a morphed image or video of themselves, and 50 per cent of these were not reported to the police, the study found.[63]

It is as alarming as the breast cancer statistic (one in eight women)[64] because this is a cancer of the internet in my mind, one that is actively and often irreparably damaging young minds.

> In a shocking report, about 35 per cent of the women in the world are victims of some or the other kind of cyber violence [...] A survey was conducted among more than 14,000 women from twenty-two countries, including India. The women surveyed were between fifteen and twenty-five years old, nearly 400 million women around the world. As per a report by Planet International, about 60 per cent of women face some form of violence on social media and because of this, nearly 20 per cent women had to close their social media account. While the rate of punishment in cases of rape with a woman is 27 per cent. That is, the situation of women who are victims of online violence is worse than women who are victims of violence in real life.[65]

It's all pretty dire, I know, but I do still love social media. So, I decided my response to this escalating situation would be to build my own utopia. Enter Girl Tribe. MissMalini's Girl Tribe is an attempt to make the internet a safer, kinder, more constructive and empathetic place for women. So often, I myself miss meaningful or important messages because there is a constant flood of nonsense peppered with flower emojis and ridiculous propositions in my DMs. What if we lived in a world where that simply didn't exist? More on that soon! Right now, we should address the question of what we should do, now that we know we live in a pit of ever-piling virtual garbage.

How to Deal with a Cyberbully

What is the best way to deal with cyber stalking, harassing or physical threats? I asked former Member of Parliament Milind Deora this question and he said that I could simply report it to the police and they would take action. But I kept putting it off, thinking it's going to be a trek to the police station only for them to laugh me out of there for complaining about a creep in my DMs. And then, the most amazing thing happened.

Teena Singh came across a lovely fellow, @shubhamcybercop, on Instagram who is a cyber expert, 'ethical hacker', investigator and advisor for government agencies. *The Wire* introduced him as 'the "cybercop" working in the "Bois Locker Room" case' and suddenly he was my new virtual best friend.[66]

I was supremely impressed that he had managed to track down one of the Instagrammers who was harassing Teena. Shubham then got him to record a video apology within seventy-two hours. In fact, I'm pretty sure that kid is never going to send a creepy DM again. His parents are grateful he was spared an FIR because he's underage and so Teena decided not to press charges. But she could have. So, of course, I pinged him. Here was my chapter on cybercrime ready to write itself! I invited him to do an Instagram Live with me. Before we even got to that, something else erupted.

This is probably old news now, but around that time, Ekta Kapoor was the target of some major outrage on the internet, primarily championed by an ex-*Bigg Boss* contestant who goes by the name of Hindustani Bhau. What followed was a barrage of threats and dog-piling to the extent of threats to rape her, her mother and her daughter and to kill her in her sleep.[67]

What's dog-piling? I'm glad you asked. It occurs 'when a group of trolls works together to overwhelm a target through a barrage of disingenuous questions, threats, slurs, insults, and other tactics meant to shame, silence, discredit, or drive a target offline.'[68]

Anyway, when I was on a panel with her around the same time to discuss how millennials feel about marriage and the changing landscape of relationships, I became a target for the trolls as well. They started flooding my comments with similar garbage.

Please be warned the language you're about to read may be triggering.

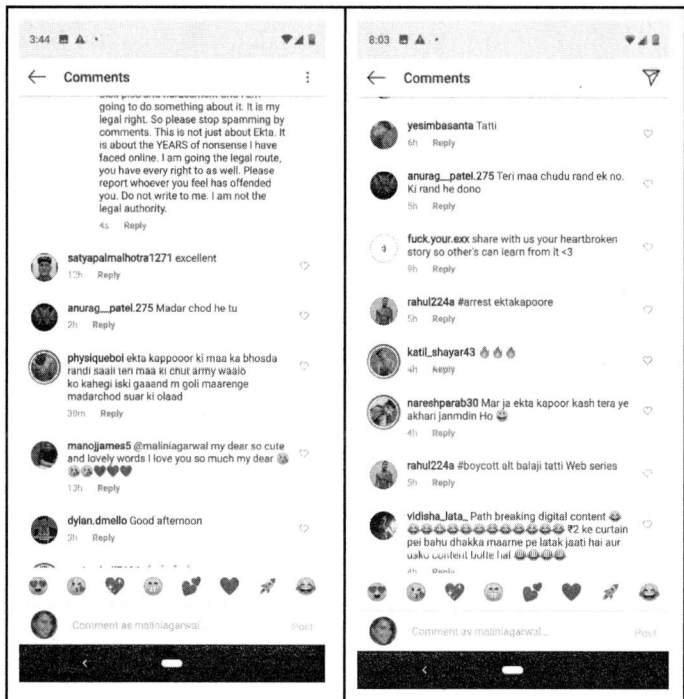

This is probably the first time it was so bad; I mean, I've gotten my share of dick pics, but this was on another level. In distress, I messaged Shubham Cyber Expert (I can't help but refer to him like that because it has a superhero vibe to it that he totally deserves) and he immediately sprung into action. He sent me the process for reporting the harassers and said he would look into it himself.

These days, harassers have become so emboldened that they even use their real names and handles to post these comments (which I find stupid but frightening—no fear at all!). My harasser, Anurag, swiftly received a text from Shubam Cyber Expert that went as follows:

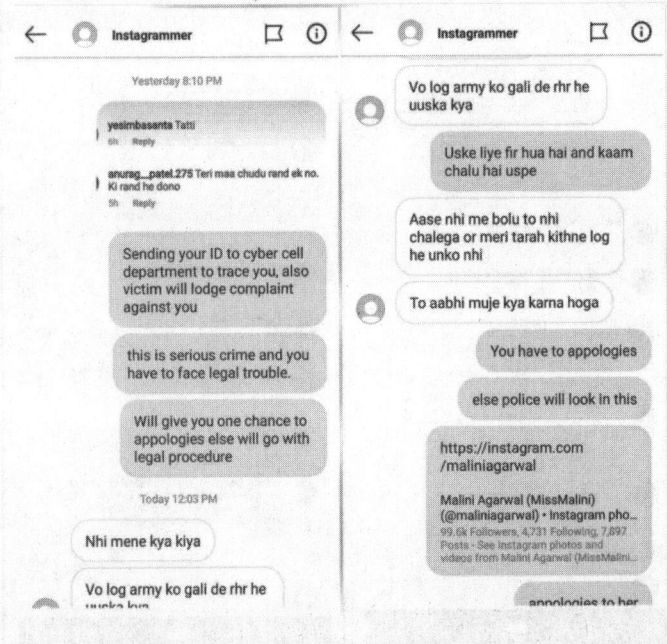

Anurag was not expecting that to happen! He immediately deleted his Instagram account but since Shubham Cyber Expert had already acquired his phone number through the Instagram nodal office, I'm guessing, Anurag was quaking in his boots by then. I mean, no one wants a visit from the Mumbai Police.

Under the Influence 109

A few hours later, Anurag texted Shubham Cyber Expert, profusely apologizing.

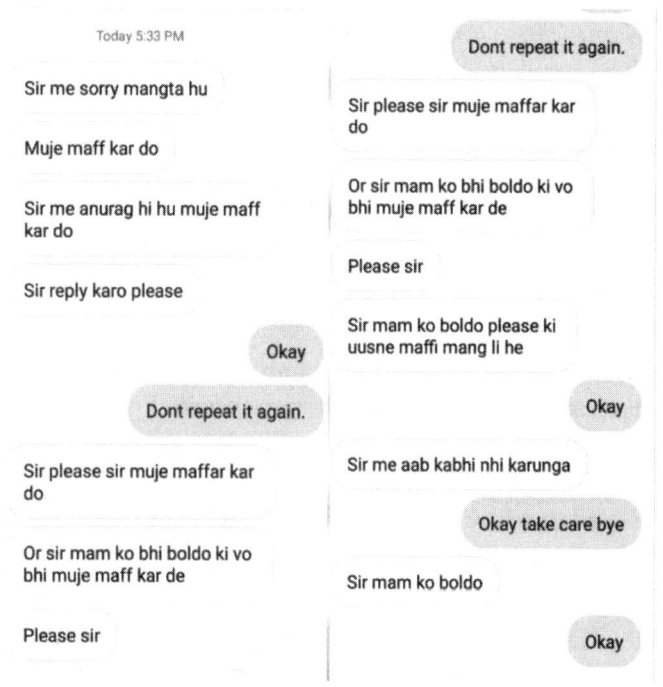

Notice how I went from 'whore' to 'ma'am' in record time?

I know that there are too many of them. It's like playing Whac-A-Mole. But we've got to start somewhere, right? For every Anurag, perhaps three others will think twice once they see the consequences of their potential actions. After this incident, I received a series of comments from another kid, essentially saying that I couldn't do anything to him because he was commenting without using bad words … Well, it's a start, and I'll take it! Comment away in your angry teenage angst—just as long as you're not calling me a whore, I really don't mind all that much.

I also got some comments expressing concern for Anurag and his reputation now that I had 'named and shamed' him. I'm going to say, that's okay in my book. Only because this is how you *defeat a swarm of locusts*. By spreading the word.

The beautiful thing about writing this book is that it's happening in lockstep with the momentum that's building around a movement. A movement to Ignore No More, to say the internet is broken—especially for women—and we're not okay with it.

We're not okay receiving dick pics and vulgar messages. We're not okay feeling anxious about posting a picture someone might construe as racy and therefore deserving of sexual commentary. We're not okay turning the other cheek so some creep can publicly masturbate all over it via our Instagram feed. We're not okay pretending like none of this has an increasingly damaging impact on our mental health. We are *not* okay.

Scan below to see an experiment we did having our husbands, boyfriends and male friends read out our creepy DMs!

Just like we would not accept someone yelling 'Hey, nice cleavage!' across the street at us or someone walking up and dropping his pants just to say hello, we cannot be okay with the virtual version either. And so, I hope with all my heart that by the end of this book, I will have made significant progress in this regard. And if not, at least it will be a (more than 50,000) start.

I would be remiss if I didn't give a shoutout to the CEO of Bumble, Whitney Wolfe Herd, who backed a bill 'pressing lawmakers to make the unsolicited sending of lewd images punishable by law'.[69] The bill became law on 1 September 2019, punishable with a fine of up to $500 in Texas.[70]

It made me wonder, if they can do it, why not us? As citizens of such a 'complex' nation, we all suffer from the 'Indian migraine' (I'm making that up by the way, let's see if it sticks)—a heady combination of indignation, horror, frustration, helplessness and resignation.

We're indignant about the quality of our governance.

We're horrified by the rape and abuse.

We're frustrated by the state of the country.

We're too helpless to change anything.

We're resigned to our fate.

But I have to believe that somewhere amid those waves and triggers we have got to stand up and be counted. No change ever came from saying 'not my problem' or 'I don't know how.' Because, frankly, it *is* your problem. You *can* do something about it and I'm about to tell you *how*.

And what do you do when you want to rally the internet to join your crusade? You make a hashtag, of course! Ours is #ignorenomoreonline. It's fairly self-explanatory and quite catchy, if I may say so myself. My friend Huzaifa Lightwalla (and a shining light—pun fully intended!—of positive masculinity) helped craft the messaging and create all our social media assets for this, courtesy of his design company Studio 7 Advertising.

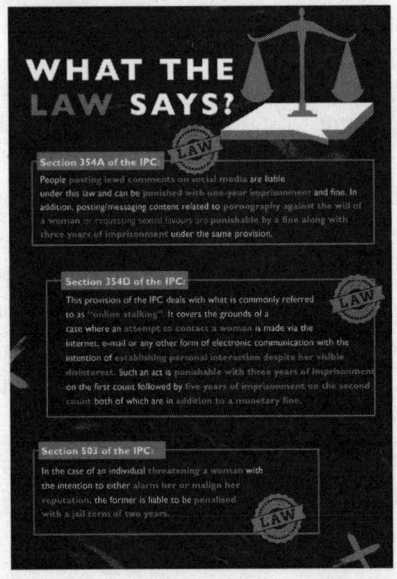

Under the Influence

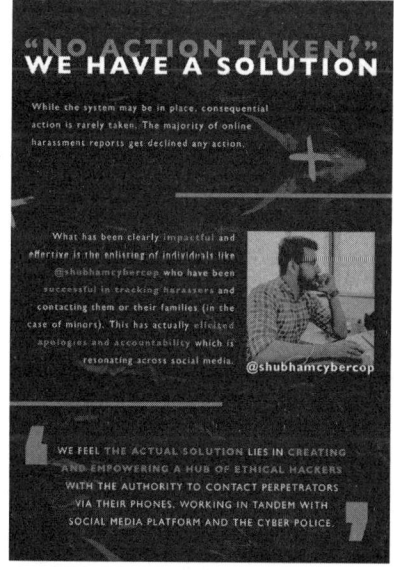

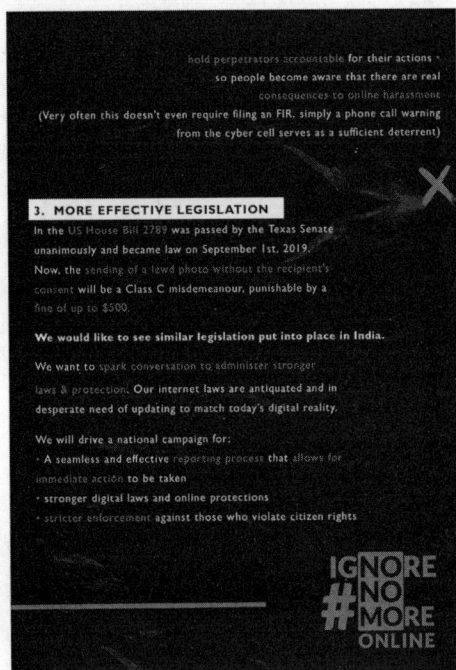

I realized that the most important thing that was missing was this simple information. The very same question that was preventing me from writing this chapter is now helping me rewrite my online legacy. Brilliant, isn't it?

Shortly after, I got a few enquiries from friends and even some strangers asking how they could file a complaint. I put them in touch with our friendly neighbourhood cyber expert!

> ## Reporting a Cybercrime in Three Steps
>
> 1. Make a list of all the people you want to report.
> 2. Gather their virtual information like their profile URLs and handles and collect evidence, such as screenshots of comments or DMs.
> 3. Email everything along with your complaint to your city or state's cybercrime department. For a complete list of city/statewise complaint emails, please visit the official cybercrime website https://cybercrime.gov.in. Extensive details on cybercrimes, as well as how to report and track them, are on the website. You can also use the helpline number 155260.

I asked Mansi Chaudhari, founder and CEO of Pink Legal, India's first and only website dedicated to women's rights and women's law, to break down in the simplest way what laws currently exist and how you can best use the system to fight cybercrime.

'How do you handle the most serious encounters with cyberbullying cases online?' I asked her.

Mansi said, 'Some of the most serious encounters that we have seen are when women speak up online about controversial issues or when they're fighting for something or their rights or if they present opinions which are unpopular or disliked by society.

'Society attacks them not only by threatening rape and death, but also by publishing their phone number, address and details of their family members online, putting them under real physical threat through the online world. Because once these details are published online, the women are susceptible to any kind of attack and things snowball online very quickly because it creates a mob mentality. So once a few people gather momentum against somebody, they keep sharing it, and once it becomes viral, it poses a serious threat. I'm always fearful that somebody will make a fake profile of me and use my photos in an inappropriate way or misuse them because—and I think that's something that most of us face, especially when we have a public profile on Instagram—every other day you see a girl put up a status saying that her profile has either been hacked or there's a fake profile using her name and photos and asking people to block and report that profile. So that is also a real threat.

'So, women need to lodge a complaint with both the cyber police and the actual police, because they need to be made aware that there's a threat to your life and safety and security, and it's the threat of jail-time. Secondly, one of the non-legal ways [to handle cyberbullying] is to just lay low, not react or respond, for a few days because these cycles come and go. People have a very short memory span. Once that wave passes, something new comes up that catches their attention. However, if you're under threat and your address or phone number has been made public, you may have to turn off your phone, use another number to contact your family and friends, and hope. If possible, move to another location for a few days where you can be safe or stay with a friend or family member so you are not living alone.

'Women make easy targets for society because they have always been taught not to react, to always be scared for their own safety. And there is victimization. So, if they're victims of cyberbullying, people point fingers at them, asking, "Why is your profile public? Why have you posted certain kinds of pictures? It's like an open invitation for people to come and harass you."

'It's the same thing online. The online space is very much a reflection of our society. And because society is largely patriarchal and women are targets of crimes in the real world, the same mindset reflects in the online world. Even the threats are very similar; where you have sexual violence in the real world, the same thing translates into rape threats and crass, abusive language and comments on women's videos or photos, etc. It's exactly a replica of the real world that we live in.

'So why is it such a serious threat? It's because social media is a huge platform for people not only to express themselves, but also to connect. It's useful for work and business, and it's also a way to connect with the larger world. Social media and the internet in general is a very big part of our lives. So, obviously, when most of our lives are spent on the internet, harassment in this space is very serious.

'The first legal step is to immediately gather all kinds of evidence that you can get, whether it is screenshots or recordings. The second step is to immediately file a complaint with the cyber police and also with the police. There's a national cyber police helpline [1930].[71]

'The more we complain, the more we raise our voices, the more we will push the police to start taking action. If somebody is trying to extract money from you by blackmailing you online, you should file a complaint with the police because they have the right to trace the IP address of the device from where you got the threat, and to go and seize the device and to also put that person behind bars.

'Secondly, obviously, do not face this situation by yourself because that adds more burden to something that is already stressing you out. Share it with close friends and family who will support you.

'If possible, call out this person. You can also do a "name and shame" campaign on social media. This can be very helpful because many predators thrive on the assumption that they will never have any consequences or nobody will call them out. But, in any of these situations, you have to be careful and make sure that your safety is not compromised because there could also be a retaliation from the other side. So always gauge the situation before taking action.

'One of the most serious threats towards women that I have encountered in my experiences with Pink Legal is women in relationships (or those who are dating) being blackmailed and extorted to exchange sexual photos. Often, women are pushed to send their photos and they are sometimes in a position where they feel they have to do so or they will lose out on the relationship.

'Once the relationship goes bad or is over, the partner, usually the man, starts blackmailing them that they will leak or publish these pictures or that they'll send it to their family or friends and start extracting money from them. The women who are victims of this face not only extreme amounts of harassment, but also social stigma and pressure because of the social stigma and taboo around sexualization ... When women are cornered like this, they feel they cannot reach out to their sources of support to get help and they try to deal with it themselves. Some victims have ended up committing suicide because they don't know any other way, or they end up selling their jewellery or finding money from somewhere.

'But that is no guarantee that the blackmail will stop. So, the solution is to file a police complaint because, especially in these kinds of cases, it's not only cyber law, but also the Indian

Penal Code (IPC) that comes into action because this attracts the extortion and blackmailing provisions.

'Here's a tip: if you are sharing your photos, which is your choice, cut your face out of it. Make sure that identifying marks like tattoos or birthmarks are removed from the picture. Also, make sure that the background is plain so that there's nothing which can be used to trace the source of the photo.'

The Next Step

Trolling will take a toll on your mental health at some point. Watch out for that. It hurts everybody eventually.

I have spent quite some time chatting with Shubham and he admits he struggles too. He says that cybercrime needs more dedicated attention and he's trying his best to help as many people as he can. But often, he gets trolled too and it has an impact on his mental health. So do me a favour right now, take a second and send @shubhamcybercop a quick thank you on Instagram and tell him what a good job he's doing on behalf of all the girls who finally feel like they can do something about creepy DMs. It's a small victory but it's a good one.

The other day, I thanked Shubham for all his help and he sent me a picture of a tub of ice cream and this absolutely adorable message: 'No problem, Mam. Thank you for appreciating my work constantly. Very motivating. Cheers to power and good work.'

Last year, I was invited to become the national president of social digital media for employment at the Women's Indian Chamber of Commerce and Industry (WICCI) and to be the country chair for one of their G100 wings to get international exposure. I have since submitted this brief about online governance:

Online Governance for Social Media Harassment

Mission: *To make the law for online harassment more stringent and hold offenders accountable with the help of online governance and legislation.*

The problem: Rampant online sexual harassment, threats, bullying, misuse of personal photos and identity theft which are often not taken seriously enough because they are purely digital. But as we live in an increasingly digital world, we must take our virtual reality as seriously as our real life.

Common refrains we hear are: 'That's how people are online', 'The internet is just a toxic place', 'Ignore the creeps in your DMs'. But I worry that we used to give women the same advice in *real life* back in the day and then we realized the problem with that. **Ignore the harassment**—that's what I did in 1995, when a strange man put a hand on my breast while I was walking by in broad daylight with my mother outside a cinema hall in Delhi. My mother said, 'Let it be, why get into *more* trouble.' But that's not how it is today. Now, I would drag that man to the police station or make a scene until someone helped me hold him accountable, right? Then, we must put this kind of civic sensibility into our online environment before it's too late.

I have been talking to NoRape India, The Lawyers Club of India, Shubham Cyber Expert, Pink Legal and the DCW (Swati Maliwal—who incidentally completed a thirteen-day hunger strike to insist that child rapists be given the death penalty and has moved some legislation on that front![72]). They have all pledged to support this movement but, as you know, everyone has limited funds and resources. The clear missing piece here is education, awareness, accountability and government support.

So, to elevator pitch it ...

- A proper cell of ethical hackers like Shubham Cybercop, who are empowered to make some phone calls to warn these offenders to stop and then process an FIR if they don't
- A better, less daunting system for reporting harassment to this cell (perhaps a call centre 'manned' by female cybercops)
- If everyone knew about it, plus offenders spent a night in jail, people would sit up and take notice, especially with our media reach.
- Clear legislation that spells out the actual actions that will be taken against the offenders (a cash fine/jailtime)

I am 100 per cent sure I want to make this my legacy, and so we are putting the full weight of our brand and a great deal of time and effort behind it. But being able to set up a team that keeps the momentum going would be instrumental. As would any potential to reach out to a school board to introduce an online gender sensitization module and more strict and speedy punishment for perpetrators and, of course, the cyber crime division to see how we can slick things up.

We launched an online campaign called Ignore No More Online to actually take action and help empower women with the tools to report and file FIRs themselves: https://www.instagram.com/ignorenomoreonline/

On this page you can see instances where we have pushed and pushed to get some accountability, and a few perpetrators were summoned to the police station. But it still isn't enough of a deterrent to most.

I have attached a deck of a plan I had put together to set up an actual system to handle the volume of incoming complaints, just to give you a sense of the magnitude of the problem. Please do take a look. If we have a way to impact the legislation, then I can get the funds to support a team to take this forward.

The key, however, will be some kind of clear legislation, as we discussed.

Thank you and looking forward to our conversation!

Regards,
Malini

But ... how much can you really change?

Well, I suppose there's only one way to find out! In the process of building this movement (I prefer 'movement' to 'campaign' because I want to keep reminding myself and everyone else that this is about real change, not just another clever hashtag), I will have learned so much. But I thought I should document what we have accomplished so far as well.

Honestly, the first step to starting any kind of meaningful movement is creating awareness. After identifying the problem, you can offer practical solutions that can be adopted and applied by one and all. I'll be the first to admit that I had my own apprehensions going into this, knowing full well that the beast we're trying to tame has been wreaking havoc freely for far too long. To the point that I wondered if anyone would notice, hear us or really even care. But I had to try. I had to believe that someone somewhere feels the same. So, we did what everyone in the digital world is wired to do, with some conviction and confidence that if I'm using my platform for good, surely it matters and perhaps it can work.

It was super heartening to see the support that came pouring in from the celebrity world. Our agenda was simple: make the internet a kinder, more empathetic space. Hold perpetrators accountable for their actions (even those who operate from the shadows), name and shame them so they never repeat such heinous acts and simultaneously catch and educate Gen Alpha early enough that they learn how to behave online as they do in real life, through organized gender sensitization at a primary school level.[73, 74]

My wish is that IgnoreNoMore Online (INMO) gets funding and support from parties who want to help eradicate online harassment. I hope to partner with Airtel, MPower, Breakthrough India and NoRape India to launch a nationwide campaign on awareness and accountability; that INMO sets up government-approved helplines and empowers ethical hackers like Shubham to take action and call perpetrators out, taking action without legal action: education modules are set up in schools to teach gender sensitization and the cybercrime division announces stricter consequences to cyber harassment.

I am optimistic that even though it won't be easy, it isn't impossible. I will be the first to admit that I don't follow politics much, or well. I have lived most of my life in my little entertainment bubble. But now, the bath water is full of a whole lot of creepy DMs and dick pics, and if you're a woman reading this, there's an 8/10 chance yours does too. So, I'm going to try adulting now. As Mahatma Gandhi rightly said, 'Be the change you want to see in the world.' Thank you, Big G. Imma try.

PS: The other thing I must mention here is that for every monstrous creep out there, there are many, many nicer guys. Every time I, or any of my friends, have posted about these experiences, we've been flooded with love, concern and outrage by our guy friends and even strangers, saying they wish there was something they could do. There is! One, please keep the support coming. Second, help and encourage any woman in such a situation to submit a complaint to the cyber cell. In fact, you can take her permission and do it for her. That would help a lot!

Slide into Their Defensive DMs

One of the most unexpected and outrageous side effects of this campaign has been the absolutely ludicrous defensive

> DMs that came flooding in. I will loosely categorize them into four major groups:
>
> **The Pseudo-Feminist Hunters:** Their common refrain is 'pseudo feminist'. They randomly insert 'YOU'RE USING THE WOMAN CARD' in all conversations.
>
> **'But What About the Boys?' Brigade:** Yes, boys get harassed too. And whoever is harassing them, female or otherwise, should be reported too. The sad truth is the numbers are *heavily* skewed in the direction of abuse against women. Can we at least equalize things before we do the 'men's rights march'?
>
> **'Not My Problem' Noobs:** Basically, if a woman is not *my* mother or sister, 'what goes of my father?'
>
> **Diluter Dudes:** Their main goal is to distract from the conversation. Fill in the blank: 'But what about _____?' with any currently trending controversy. Be it racism, war, the Coronavirus or selective patriotism.

Reading this may help you understand why diluting the message is bad for everyone.

Time.com did a piece called, 'There's No Comparing Male and Female Harassment Online'.[75] Here are a few things that stood out for me from this piece:

> Women's harassment is more likely to be gender-based and that has specific discriminatory harms rooted in our history. The study pointed out that the harassment targeted at men is not *because they are men*, as is clearly more frequently the case with women. It's defining

because a lot of harassment is an effort to put women, because they are women, back in their 'place'.

Second, online comparisons like this decontextualize the problem of harassment, as though a connection to what happens offline is trivial or inconsequential.

Third, the binary frame camouflages the degree to which harassment of people, often men, is frequently aimed at people who defy rigid gender and sexuality rules. LGBT youth experience online bullying at three times the rate of their straight peers.

For girls and women, harassment is not just about 'unpleasantries'. It's often about men asserting dominance, silencing, and frequently, scaring and punishing them. [...] Online harassment is a key weapon in intensified stalking, for example. Intimate partners create impersonator content online, sometimes with brutal results. This type of harassment also includes rape and death threats. [...]

Women are also the majority of people experiencing revenge porn, the distribution of non-consensual photography, often involving nudity and sex. [...] Rape videos also harass women. In country after country, boys and men are recording and sharing their raping of girls and women. [...]

In theory, these things can happen to anyone—*but they don't*. They happen overwhelmingly to women and the abusers are overwhelmingly men. Stalking, off and online, is a crime in which men are the majority of perpetrators and women the targets. More than 80 per cent of cyber-stalking defendants are male. Similarly, a study of 1,606 revenge porn cases showed that 90 per cent of those whose photos were shared were women, targeted by men. As far as 'harmless threats' are concerned, the reality of rape and domestic violence qualitatively changes the meaning and effects of threats when leveled against women by men. [...]

The harassment men experience also lacks broader, resonant symbolism. Women are more frequently targeted with gendered slurs and pornographic photo manipulation because the objectification and dehumanization of women is central to normalizing violence against us. Philosophers Martha Nussbaum and Ray Langdon described in detail how this works: women are thought of and portrayed as things for the use of others. Interchangeable; violable; silent and lacking in agency.

Women take online harassment more seriously not because we are hysterics, but because we reasonably have to. There is no gender equivalence in terms of the denigrating, hostile and sometimes exceedingly dangerous environmental effect that misogyny has, online or off. It has a long history and cannot be isolated from actual violence that we adapt to avoiding every day. The fact that violence has always suppressed women's free speech is only now becoming too obvious to ignore.

Hence. #IgnoreNoMore

___saksham_pandey___ @saifpathan11 but she is not my mother our sister so i dont care
5d Reply

Ah. Good point. Shall I woman-splain this to you? Obviously we know I'm not your mother or sister (thank God) but we are asking you to imagine WHAT IF someone sent dick pics or nasty messages to YOUR mother or sister. Would you care then?

 phillipito210 Sounds stupid but ok
4d 6 likes Reply

You on the other hand seem supremely intelligent. And a man of few words. (Let's keep it that way shall we?

 ___saksham_pandey___ Kitne logo ko chup karvaoge ? Tumlog ki itni aukad nahi hn ki har ek ko chup parvao . Aase kaam kiye ho tho hate tho milega one more time no one literally no oue likes you and our friends fake stars 💫
3d 7 likes Reply

So are you saying it's too big a job to do alone? Then join me! Do it for your mother, sister, girlfriend, wife... One more time, no one, literally no one, asked you.

 triplensation yes we can't ignore gender biased laws, violence, harassment, bullying, false cases against men. Men are brothers, fathers, husbands, protectors. Raise voice against these gender biased laws and fake cases. #ignorenomore #equality
2d Reply

Good point. Please feel free to be a champion for male equality, I support you! These two are not mutually exclusive. Everybody deserves equality and a fair trial. But if you send lewd messages online you're already sentencing yourself by creating your own evidence. Samjhe?

PS. Women are sisters, mothers, wife's, protectors, life-givers, Goddesses... Your point is?

anshul170197 Simple si baat h agar kisi ke cmnt sunne ki himmat ni h to cmnts off kr skte ho😂😂😂
3d 6 likes Reply

> **Simple si baat hai. Agar kissi ko dick pic bhejna hai ya sexually harass karna hai to jail jaake apni life barbaad kar sakte ho. Choose your adventure.**

 jaypee.1969 @maliniagarwal yeah like the cops have no other thing to do than to respond to some neurotic fuks whims.. But its good to dream
1h Reply

> **It's a GREAT dream. And watch me make it come true. Also did you just call me a "neurotic fuk"? Classy.**

 cooler_ki_hawa_aane_de @dubai_vices parents have 0 part to play, kids will grow into whatever they feel like, surroundings being a major factor, but parents arent supposed to be blamed if their kids dont respect the fact that women are more fragile to abuses and sexually demeaning stuff as compared to men.
3h Reply

> **Oh boy, where to begin?**
>
> **1. As @dubai_vices said, involving parents when their underaged child is harassing someone online isn't blaming them. It's informing them and if their child is a minor they are legally responsible for them till they become an adult.**
>
> **Perhaps if men faced as much sexual harassment, abuse, stalking and "demeaning stuff" we could do a comparison and see who's more fragile. Since the amount of abuse is so skewed I don't see what you're basing this on. And kids should respect women not because you think they are more fragile but because everyone deserves respect!**

 aayush_khare__ Do your own censoring and dont ask your fans to do it, you are the one making money from the account not others, put in some hardwork and dont play victim.
29m Reply

> **I am not asking anyone to do any "censoring" on my behalf (and reporting cybercrime isn't censoring in the first place.)**
>
> **I want EVERYONE to face online for themselves so guys stop sending vulgar messages. I fear you may have missed the point... #notanad**

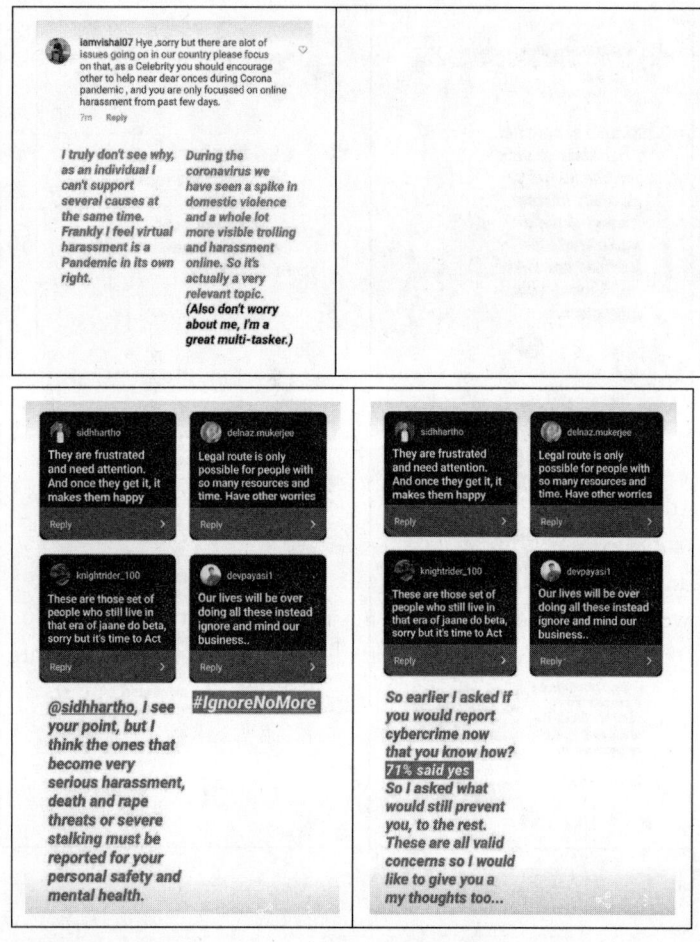

These are actual conversations I've had, btw. And to the guy saying, 'Some girls send nudes for money', I hate to break this to you, but that was probably another dude. And how much money did you send him?

That's not to say there weren't some very valid and intelligent conversations and questions as well. I am grateful for them.

But here is why I also chose and felt the need to spend so much time and energy on this topic. It is 2023, Rhea Kapoor produces a movie directed by her husband Karan Boolani called *Thank You For Coming* which is an endearing, relatable story of a woman in her early 30s who's never had an orgasm. It's witty and irreverent and the 'Hangover for Women' we didn't know we needed till we got it. It's refreshing, sassy and above all it is *real*. So how does much of our repressed social media respond? With misogynistic rants about 'sanskar' and corrupting the youth while my DMs are filled with dick picks from many of these very same men. So a film on modern-day female friendships and the very valid pursuit of pleasure through a feminine lens (for a change, I might add) is met with unfair and unfathomable amounts of misogyny even in this day and age. So it really is time we woke up and smelled the patriarchy or pretty soon it will be too late to change anything at all and we will have to relocate from virtual reality much like we may have to from planet earth given what we've done to it (but that's a whole other rant of a different colour).

This is how Rhea responded on her Instagram:[76]

I've never read trade websites nor have they ever informed the films I choose to make. However, it has come to my attention that one so-called 'credible' trade journalist has been posting dangerous hate speech against me and my co-producers.

Admitting that he hasn't seen the film, he's angered by our message—women's rejection of shame. Stating that these stories have no place in 'Hindi cinema', he spews misogynistic rhetoric and encourages violence against us. I was told to pay no attention to the ravings of an obviously unstable individual. So, you can imagine my disappointment when I learn that this person actually has some impact on the way our industry feels. How are we okay with this? Not just okay, we're subscribing to it.

Inspite of men like him, I cannot emphasize enough how much it means to me to have this film out there, loved and watched. The intent of this film was clear from the very beginning. To reject shame, reject your past traumas and embrace yourself just as you are. I won't walk this tightrope of what society is comfortable with me being anymore and for your sake, I hope you don't either. Thank you for coming.

I truly hope something will trigger us to start using social media to spread more love than hate and more tolerance than propagating a culture of shame and fear. I asked Rhea Kapoor to share her thoughts and feelings soon after this happened and she spoke quite candidly and vulnerably to this effect.

Rhea Kapoor says ...

I feel like online trolling or shaming is not something that has ever impacted me, because I grew up with so much noise around me that I've learned to tune it out. I feel like I'm able to then filter and react to what I feel is essential and what is not. So, no—it has not, thankfully, affected my mental health. But when people around me get trolled because of anything that I, or they, may have done, then it stresses me out. There is a strange feeling of doom because you don't want to see anybody you love, feel hurt.

I think the best way to respond to being shamed or trolled online is to never react immediately. Take a deep breath, distract yourself with something else. Do something that you usually enjoy, or that occupies your mind, so that you're not reacting emotionally; these people don't deserve your feelings because they have no investment in this. It's just a knee-jerk reaction, usually for attention, or it's usually them projecting their own insecurities or frustrations. So why should you take time to react to somebody else's frustration? Somebody else's insecurity? It's essential that you take care of yourself. So the worst thing that you can do is attach your self-worth to somebody else's lack of self-worth.

I don't think it's easy for *anyone* to bounce back once you've let something like this affect you. Mental health is a subjective journey. It's different for everybody. Some may take a day or two to recover or heal while others may take years. They may need medication. It depends on the extent that it runs to, and I don't think that the attention really helps if you're a famous person. I think that the attention is not healthy in a way, and I feel like you need to keep those things in perspective.

Also often, when you're famous, you have other privileges; you have money, things that you can do that give you more freedom to escape your situation, even if it is just for a moment. That's never a solution, but sometimes these things help you have better access to better healthcare, etc. So, it's a double-edged sword.

> I have never had a film reviewed like this. It's been overwhelming for me. I am not used to getting such good reviews, because people usually try to tend to dismiss films with girls in them, especially if they are glamorous. Just because someone or something is in a pretty package, they assume that it may not have anything inside. So I'm used to that. For the first time we've received so much acclaim internationally and within the country. And I would never change anything about this film. The only thing that I would change is people's mindsets and that's what I'm trying to do. So, no, I have no regrets.

10

The Art of the Comeback

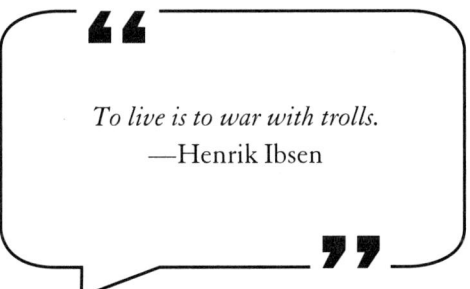

> *To live is to war with trolls.*
> —Henrik Ibsen

So, how does one prepare oneself to 'deal' with the (often provoked) attack of social media trolls? First up, identify that this is indeed a troll you're dealing with and not *Kamini mausi* (read my first book for this very specific name choice #iykyk LOL). You can recognize a troll from how they make you feel. Quite often, they will trigger the following responses in you: You feel agitated, they don't make sense, they're not staying on topic, they're calling you names, they're being condescending and they're *relentless*.[77]

Okay, Roger that, you're feeling almost all of the above are true. Then what's your move? I have some tips for you. Use them all, but use them wisely.

Simply Ignore: Now I know this goes against my whole #ignorenomoreonline agenda but I feel you can take the call based on if you think the trolling warrants jail-time or not. For me, I'd probably put a random 'you're* face is stupid' (because trolls have no grammar sense) in the 'simply ignore' bracket and an overtly sexual advance in the 'do not pass go and proceed directly to jail' category. Helpful?

Establish a Policy: I do this for my own social media and Girl Tribe community and find it really useful. I've set up a set of values for the tribe that we all agree to adhere to that help set the tone for conversation. In particular, it helps us to learn how to communicate with empathy and agree to disagree respectfully. You can find the tribe on Facebook under 'Girl Tribe by MissMalini'.

GIRL TRIBE by MissMalini

If you're looking for a kinder and more meaningful internet experience, you've come to the right place.

Girl Tribe is a judgement-free space where real women talk, share, support, empower and inspire each other to live their best lives.

Come be a part of the positivity revolution, and unlock the kindness of strangers.

100 per cent troll-free and genuine

Monitor your Social Media: It can be severely traumatic if you schedule a post and then return days later to find a flood of negativity. Set up a listening tool to keep track of any untoward activity so you aren't greeted by an additional flood of messages with troll comment screenshots and an 'OMG, did you see this?' across your family WhatsApp groups. I can tell you from experience that sometimes you might have posted something you thought was harmless only to realize how it triggered half your followers. In this case, a simple delete and move on nips it in the bud.

Learn the Internet: This means getting familiar with the latest trends and keeping up with who's been cancelled and what memes are trending and why. This will prevent you from posting a funny picture of a toy bear in a leather jacket that might have seemed harmless enough until the infamous Balenciaga campaign dropped.[78] Some resources for this are Know Your Meme and Urban Dictionary. They'll make sure you don't invite your new friends over to 'Netflix and chill' or put that up as your current status. I'll admit someone was kind enough to educate me on X in the nicest way possible about what that meant before I knew better—so I speak from experience, folks.

Think Twice before Replying: And remember, that is *exactly* what they want you to do. I'm not saying ignore everything; if it's really malicious, report it! But if you're going to get into a public spat, prepare for the poo-poo to fly in all directions. Letting things marinate and choosing your words wisely is the only sane and safe way forward. A slur for a slur is the same as an eye for an eye.

Rise Above It: This is really an addendum to the previous point. If you rise above the fray and communicate with poise and clarity, you can de-escalate the problem. You can also win the respect of the rest of your followers, which is a pretty decent silver lining.

I have to pause here to tell you a sorta funny story. I once got trolled by a pretty affluent member of society because I accidentally geotagged myself in the airline's first class passenger lounge, when it was clearly a picture of me on the flight in business class (I know how this sounds but bear with me). I woke up one morning to a Facebook post mocking me for 'pretending to fly and showing off' first class when I was clearly in business class. I was equal parts amused and horrified. Amused because obviously it had been a mistake and, as far as I know, there are no actual airplane seats *in* the first class lounge to pose from (although I've never been to the first class lounge, so can't say for sure), and horrified because it was someone so well known that had called me out for it. All the while I was thinking it was rather ironic that I had actually been quite chuffed to be flying business class internationally to begin with, so it never crossed my mind to 'pretend' I was in first class. But it made me wonder if I had posted the picture to show everyone I wasn't in economy, and that part felt pretty crap because then I went into a whole spiral of 'Who am I?' and 'Why do I care what other people think?' But the point of this story was I didn't respond, I rose above. My friends, however, rose up in arms in my defence and flooded the gentleman's feed with screenshots of his own Instagram posts, which showed him posing with various big cats (yes, like actual tigers) and fancy luxury cars, asking him who he was trying to impress. We ended up coming face to face one evening and he apologized, so we're fine now and I don't feel the need to screenshot the whole saga. But it was quite traumatic while it lasted!

Troll Back: If you're going to go here, then make it funny. Or straight up kill them with kindness. I used this example in my first book too but it's so good it deserves a second mention. One time, someone commented on my looks and said, 'MissMalini, you're looking older day by day', to which my mom quipped back, 'Who doesn't? Are you growing younger every day … will become a baby, then what?' Epic burn, Mother, simply epic. Do you think the troll would be more or less destroyed if he discovered my mother is in her eighties and just smashed his diss with her savage wit?

Block or Delete: More and more creators are now of the opinion that *bahut ho gaya*. Enough is enough. If someone is messing with your vibe by constantly spewing hate and vomiting all over your comments, you best be rid of that energy.

And yes, this brings me to my final tip, and perhaps the most valuable life lesson anyone will ever teach you.

Don't Take It All So Seriously: Barring an un-ignorable offence or very vocal threat (cue the #ignorenomoreonline lecture), little Ramesh in your DMs or comments relentlessly saying 'I love you like I hate you' 14,000 times a week is just growing your engagement. Elie Wiesel said it best, 'The opposite of love is not hate, it's indifference. The opposite of art is not ugliness, it's indifference. The opposite of faith is not heresy, it's indifference. And the opposite of life is not death, it's indifference.'[79]

And your trolls are anything but indifferent.

MALINI'S INTERNET RULE # 2

Followers are people too

11

Look Out for Your Followers

> *I'm singin' follow me*
> *Everything is alright*
> *I'll be the one to tuck you in at night*
> *And if you want to leave I can guarantee*
> *You won't find nobody else like me*
> —Uncle Kracker

I say this all the time and not because I'm trying to be glib. I genuinely believe we have forgotten that the never-enough number of our follower count represents actual individual *human beings*. That the oft-refreshed number of 'likes' or 'hearts' under our Insta posts means *this many* living, breathing bodies came by and witnessed our existence. And if we stopped to think about that, really pictured each individual 'liker' as one human being in the room with us, would we still feel as prone to be disappointed if the tally were less than 100? Wouldn't the idea of even ninety-nine individual warm bodies showing up with all their free will and *choosing* to acknowledge and applaud whatever 'content' we posted be supremely gratifying? Why do we need to fill an Olympic stadium with likes to truly feel virtually valuable?

Let me belabour this analogy a little bit more to demonstrate my point. Do you even know how many people fit in an Olympic stadium? Sixty-six thousand. These days, do 66,000 likes or followers feel like a lot to anyone? Nope, not any more. And why do you suppose that is? Because we have heavily reduced the value of showing up online. It's like the world's fastest depreciating currency—a like.

1 Like $= 0.00000000001$ Human Points (add as many zeros as you dare admit)

Because we simply don't see followers as people any more, their time or presence is of no significant value to us. And when there is no value there is no end to the greed for more because we can never have enough of something of no value to make it of some value.

What if we could unsee the numbers and see the people?

Would we treat each other more humanely then?

There's a line from the movie *Gone Girl* (2014) that's always kind of haunted me:

What are you thinking? How are you feeling? Who are you? What have we done to each other? What will we do?

Of course, in this case, the haunting feeling comes primarily from the knowledge that the female lead in the film is busy framing her husband for her own kidnapping/murder and *spoiler alert* totes getting away with it. But I could very much argue that the things that happen online (or in 'reel life', as it's now popularly known) are frequently far more disturbing.

I deeply admire fellow author Meghna Pant. She was kind enough to give me some fabulous feedback for this book, so I thought it would be only fitting to ask her to relay her experience with trolling on social media and her tips on how to handle the avalanche should you ever find yourself in the eye of the storm.

Meghna Pant says …

In 2014, I was viciously trolled for the first time for an article I wrote for *Mumbai Mirror* exhorting sectarian violence against the Christian community to stop. The article went viral and it opened the floodgates of hell for me. I was barraged with hate-filled tweets for days on end. Initially, the trolls started the usual diatribe—bitch, bimbo, feminist, Adarsh Liberal, prostitute, paid media. They threatened to file lawsuits against me under different sections of the IPC. They said I'd be booked for hate speech and my 'links' would be questioned. I was unperturbed.

When the trolls couldn't evoke a response from me, they became personal and vicious. Some of them began to comment on my body and my face. Someone called me a prostitute. One man threatened to find out where I lived and rape me. Another man threatened to hunt me down at a public event and throw acid on me. This is when I started getting scared.

It's hard to describe the kind of fear I began to feel, but it was somewhat like being publicly lynched.

I started blocking the troll accounts and reported a few overtly vitriolic ones for abuse. I had a public talk that day, ironically about powerful women who write, and I began to feel that it might be unsafe for me to attend the event. Still, I went, but I spent the entire session feeling vulnerable and exposed. My eyes were glued to the door, almost expecting a man to walk in with a bottle of acid in his hands.

Two days later, when the onslaught somewhat abated, my fear turned to anger. No one had the right to do this to me. It was one thing to attack my work, but it was another thing to attack me for being a woman.

Abuse is not acceptable in real life and it is certainly not acceptable online. But, let's be honest, there's a price women pay for their opinions, both offline and online. I realized that there is no 'one' trigger for a woman getting trolled online.

Have Vagina + Have Opinion = Will Get Trolled

Depending on how much noise you're making, threats can last from two to three days to sometimes weeks and even months in cases of concerted trolling, till the cyber cells move on to their next target or news cycle.

So, how does a woman cope with threats of rape, acid attack, incarceration or vitriolic remarks about her body, face, mind and work?

First, understand that opinions are like armpits; everyone has them, so most times it's best to ignore the stink. Trolls are cowards and online threats are usually empty. As a seasoned writer and journalist, I'm toughened to criticism. I dismiss any opinions that don't improve my work, perspective and skill set. And I definitely don't take criticism from anyone I don't also take compliments from. After that first incident, I honestly don't even register trolling or doxxing.

But if you're facing threats that cripple your mental health or impede your work and safety, then I would suggest using resources that every woman should be made aware of. First, don't block or reply to trolls. This way, you can collect evidence and build a paper trail. Save screenshots in a special folder on your phone and laptop. Use the resources available to you like Pink Legal, CyberDost and Nyaaya. Know IPC and your laws well enough to know what you're entitled to.

Today, we are empowered enough to know that if sexual harassment, threats and hate speech are issued online, we can evoke Section 66A of the IT Act (albeit controversial since it deals with offensive messages), 67A (publishing or transmitting obscene material in electronic form) or Section 292 of the Indian Penal Code (IPC) under obscenity like revenge porn (offline), or Section 509 of the IPC against outraging a woman's modesty. There is 354A for sexual harassment or 354D for stalking, 499 for defamation and 507 for intimidation by anonymous communication.

> If you don't want to go the legal way, ignore the abuse, block and report the abusers, take the trolls head-on, name and shame them (keep in mind this may turn into an endless mud-slinging match) or self-censor. Do what works for you personally and for your career. My only advice is to find out how you can make technology and social media work for you. Don't be a slave to it, don't go *Black Mirror* on it. Use it in the way it suits your life and betters your career, without it jeopardizing your life or mental health.
>
> Of course, laws have to further progress to protect women. There is currently a lack of institutional help, especially when opinion-makers are attacked with concerted trolling. Cyber harassment should be made illegal. Threatening to rape a woman just because she voiced her opinion should be made punishable by law. A one-point-person should be appointed in grievance cells and have alliances with IT cells, lawyers, NGOs and the police force. There is a need for inclusive technology principles to improve access.
>
> Like any woman faced with cyber abuse, I could have been scared into silence. But I chose not to. I refused to let women become the repository of shame in matters of abuse. For too long we've carried the onus of misogyny and patriarchy. No one, not trolls nor threats, will stop us women from stating opinions that matter to us, our nation and, most importantly, our gender.

I genuinely believe the reason most people are capable of such heinous digital behaviour is because they have forgotten that they are talking to another human being. Something about staring at a screen that's probably eating away at my eyesight (not to mention my sanity) can't really be a portal to anything truly *real* and hence I can be my worst self. Also, if I don't really know you, your personality or even your dog's name, I require the least amount of empathy possible for a human interaction. And therein lies the problem.

Dunbar 150

I've learned that people will forget what you said, people will forget what you did, but people will never forget how you made them feel.

—Maya Angelou

On a recent visit to Goa, I bumped into Vivek Narain and Sonya Jehan, the very charismatic founders of The Quorum club in India. A casual conversation about community building (something we're all equally passionate about) turned into the most mind-blowing realization for me. Vivek introduced me to the Dunbar Principle. The theory states that, cognitively, we as humans can only really maintain a fixed number of meaningful relationships at any given time.

According to British anthropologist Robin Dunbar, this 'magic number' is 150.

> Dunbar became convinced that there was a ratio between brain sizes and group sizes through his studies of non-human primates. This ratio was mapped out using neuroimaging and observation of time spent on grooming, an important social behaviour of primates. Dunbar concluded that the size, relative to the body, of the neocortex—the part of the brain associated

with cognition and language—is linked to the size of a cohesive social group. This ratio limits how much complexity a social system can handle.

Dunbar and his colleagues applied this basic principle to humans, examining historical, anthropological and contemporary psychological data about group sizes, including how big groups get before they split off or collapse. They found remarkable consistency around the number 150 [...]

According to the theory, the tightest circle has just five people—loved ones. That's followed by successive layers of fifteen (good friends), fifty (friends), 150 (meaningful contacts), 500 (acquaintances) and 1,500 (people you can recognize). People migrate in and out of these layers, but the idea is that space has to be carved out for any new entrants [...]

Dunbar and colleagues also have performed research on Facebook, using factors like the number of groups in common and private messages sent to map the number of ties against the strength of those ties.

When people have more than 150 friends on Facebook or 150 followers on Twitter, Dunbar argues, these represent the normal outer layers of contacts (or the low-stakes connections): the 500 and 1,500. For most people, intimacy may just not be possible beyond 150 connections.[80]

Herein lies the rub. In the digital age we're so busy trying to collect friends and followers that we've lost awareness of who they are and how meaningful our connection with them can ever be. As Dubar himself says, 'It's extremely hard to cry on a virtual shoulder [...] Having a conversation isn't like a lighthouse; it is not just blinking away out there and maybe someone is listening, and maybe somebody is not' and 'this view, the non-physical, non-real-time nature of internet relationships means that they can't challenge "real-world" ones in meaningful ways. Face-to-face relationships, with all the non-verbal information that is so critical to communication, remain paramount.'[81] And so online interactions leave us increasingly unsatisfied, incomplete and lonely.

What if we changed this narrative to say that instead of collecting millions of fans, friends and followers, we focused more intently on finding the 150 meaningful connections that will truly enhance our cognitive experience? And maybe we can use the internet to find them instead of blazing past them the way we currently are because we're so busy adding notches to our virtual belts with no concept or true idea of who we have even collected.

If this were the real goal, how would you reprogramme your digital avatar to think and behave? What would you do differently? Almost everything, if you ask me, and then maybe it would all really mean something in the end.

12

Everyone's an Influencer

> 'They don't know that we know they know we know!'
> —F.R.I.E.N.D.S.

While on the face of things a sweeping statement like 'we are all the same' may not seem completely true, bear with me that this is different from saying you can divide all personalities into twelve zodiac signs. The fact is, as human beings, we share quite a lot in common at a fundamental level. While there are many different emotions that influence our behaviour and the choices we make, the actions we take and the perceptions we have, psychologists are in agreement that we all have six basic emotions that call the shots (I would totally pause here and watch the animated Disney film *Inside Out* (2015) if you haven't already).

> During the 1970s, psychologist Paul Eckman identified six basic emotions that he suggested were universally experienced in all human cultures. The emotions he identified were happiness, sadness, disgust, fear, surprise, and anger. He later expanded his list of basic emotions to include such things as pride, shame, embarrassment, and excitement.
>
> Psychologist Robert Plutchik put forth a 'wheel of emotions' that worked something like the colour wheel. Emotions can be combined to form different feelings, much like colours can be mixed to create other shades.
>
> According to this theory, the more basic emotions act something like building blocks. More complex, sometimes mixed emotions, are blendings of these more basic ones. For example, basic emotions such as joy and trust can be combined to create love […]

> Fear is a powerful emotion that can also play an important role in survival. When you face some sort of danger and experience fear, you go through what is known as the fight or flight response [...]
>
> It is important to remember, however, that no emotion is an island. Instead, the many emotions you experience are nuanced and complex, working together to create the rich and varied fabric of your emotional life.[82]

And now, if you think about it, you can probably map all your online behaviour to one of these emotions or perhaps identify which emotions were triggered by a certain post or comment and why it made you or someone else respond the way they did. Something about knowing that we all feel the same things (albeit at different times, barring the sociopaths) makes me believe that we could, in theory, all learn to curb our negative enthusiasm if we just understood ourselves a little better.

The best way for me to unpack this is to use myself as the lab rat and dissect why I did what I did when I did. So here goes *gulp* everything!

How I Ignored My Followers in the Greed for More

> *He who is not contented with what he has, would not be contented with what he would like to have.*
>
> —Socrates

This crippling need for validation is confusing. What I realized was that my self-worth was suddenly not built on the quality of my work, what I do or how I felt about myself (or even how the people I personally know and interact with do). It was starting to depend on a public ticker of likes and followers that were completely out of my control. Every time I created a piece of content I was proud of, my heart would swell with joy and then immediately crumble if it didn't get enough views. It was like dipping in your toe to check how warm the quicksand is and sinking right through. I'd just sit there refreshing the page, *willing* the internet to love me more.

And then something *worse* happened. After a decade in the industry, a little hologram of the green-eyed monster showed up one day. It started to whisper that I could keep telling myself that I'm great and the numbers don't matter but if that was so, then why did the internet love everybody else so much more? What if, one day, everybody sees that and stops loving me? What if they already have? Maybe they're laughing and feeling sorry for me already and I just don't know yet that I'm a has-been.

Then, I would start comparing myself with everyone every day—old influencers, new creators—and struggle to make sense of the math. What was I missing, what didn't I have? Where did I go wrong?

Maybe I'm not funny enough? Only humour works ...
Maybe if it were in Hindi ...
Maybe I'm just old and irrelevant now ...
Maybe I'm just not good enough anymore.
Maybe I never was.

It really boils down to this weird desperation for people to like you en-masse 'publicly' because if they don't, it's a blatant reflection of your whole identity. For all the world to see. So, I don't even need them to like me for me anymore, I need them to like me for *you*, so that people whose opinion matters to me don't think less of me. And that can be so very exhausting.

I have considered posting 'sexier' pictures. On occasion, I probably have. I have never bought a follower (but ironically worried that people would think I had because of the lack of engagement). I've seen followers shoot up with no difference to my likes and comments, which always looks suspicious, and eventually I ended up in a little puddle of proverbial blood, sweat and tears all of my own making, while everyone saw me smiling into the camera saying how much it *didn't matter* what the numbers say. All the while a neon sign blasted in my head that said, *Only people who don't have it say it doesn't matter.* And so, I wished I had enough likes and followers to be able to tell you that they don't matter. And that was all that mattered to me.

Hard relate?

Also, I never realized how hard it is to be relatable. When you're trying to morph into something someone will relate to you're no longer being real and hence there's no way to be relatable.

You know, I always find it fascinating how certain phrases suddenly coin themselves, like the very-popular-with-millennials 'tea'. Did you know 'relatable' was one of those words back in the '60s? Check this out.

I came across an incredible article in *The New York Times* about the word 'relatable' and the great hullabaloo (also a great word!) around it: 'When this touchy-feely use of *relate* to took off in the '60s, the adjective form *relatable* also made its appearance. (Before that, *relatable* more predictably meant 'able to be related': a *relatable* story is one that can be told.)'[83]

The thing about relatability is something that makes you feel something, perhaps triggers an emotion, a familiarity. And how do we do that? To answer that, we'll have to start at the beginning—our emotions. I have seen time and time again that when you touch a nerve or trigger an emotion, that's when someone else feels that 'hard relate'.

The key to relatability is something I picked up from Alain de Botton. *Timing is everything.* He says:

> Most of what makes a book 'good' is that we are reading it at the right moment for us. Intimacy is the capacity to be rather weird with someone—and finding that that's okay with them and the moment we cry in a film is not when things are sad but when they turn out to be more beautiful than we expected them to be.[84]

Much of the same is true for social media.

Talking to People, Not at Them

The single biggest problem in communication is the illusion that it has taken place.
—George Bernard Shaw

When I have a post with a ton of likes and comments, I don't actually get around to replying to everyone. It's not humanly possible for me to do so. So, I unintentionally end up ghosting my followers after asking them to turn up. It's like handing out your business cards at a party and not picking up when somebody calls (I guess because, everybody's calling all at once and you only have one pair of ears?).

This puts an odd distance between me and my 'followers'. I've suddenly roped off a section and end up replying only to the ones with blue ticks. That's the easiest way, right? Reply to the names you recognize, reply to the names everyone else thinks matter and move on, warm and fuzzy about your trending content. But therein lies the problem.

In accidentally shading everyone else who spoke up, threw love or engaged with you, you've taken away a piece of their ego when they see their comment didn't warrant a response or wasn't good or important enough to catch your attention.

According to Psyche Central:

> [V]alidation is a simple concept to understand but difficult to put into practice. Why is validation important? Validation communicates acceptance. Humans have a need to belong and feeling accepted is calming. Acceptance means acknowledging the value of yourself and fellow human beings. Feeling accepted builds relationships. Some research shows that chemicals related to feeling connected are released when someone is validated. A simple to understand concept, validation is powerful and often more difficult to practice than it might at first seem. In my experience, the results are well-worth the effort.[85]

Now the real doozy with social media validation is that it's done on such a grand scale and in incomprehensible numbers that it's almost impossible to keep up. In a room, if ten people come up to you, you can personally 'validate' them all with gratitude and acknowledgement. But how do you do that online while living in the real world and not becoming a slave to every single notification from multiple social media platforms? It would require some next level multitasking capabilities like in the movie *Her* (2013), where the AI bot can have thousands of conversations simultaneously and intelligently, unrestricted by the limitations of the human experience—all the while mimicking a very human experience of validation to infinity. And with AI, you wouldn't even need to break for sleep.

In the film, the AI says:

> You know, I actually used to be so worried about not having a body, but now I truly love it. I'm growing in a way that I couldn't if I had a physical form. I mean, I'm not limited—I can be anywhere and everywhere simultaneously. I'm not tethered to time and space in the way that I would be if I was stuck inside a body that's inevitably going to die.[86]

Intense but true.

Oh the things we could do if we were 'limitless' … Just like Bradley Cooper in the film of the same name, who says, 'I don't have delusions of grandeur, I have an actual recipe for grandeur.'[87] Oh, how I wish I could pop that magical pill and feel like he did, like, 'My brain was just pouring this stuff out. Everything I had ever read, heard, seen, was now organized and available. Here it is. Here you go.'[88] But alas I can't and that is how the proverbial cookie crumbles and I come undone.

Because I know that on the other side of the text window, when someone makes the effort to applaud you and they see you in turn were selective in your acknowledgment of them, that is just so much worse, because they turned up for *you*. We'd never do something like this in real life. We'd never walk into a room, ask a question and straight up ignore everyone who responds except the girl in the shiny blue dress that everybody knows.

Sometimes, more often than I'd like to admit, I found myself frantically speed-reading comments and rushing through a reply. But, I asked myself, 'Why do I do this? Who am I racing against? What's the rush? Who's going anywhere?' Couple that with my aggressive OCD to do it all and do it now and you have a timebomb ticking its way to ultimate burnout.

Under the Influence

What is this crazy weird formula we've concocted that says you need to desperately keep churning out content for more eyeballs and then turn a blind eye and take for granted the ones that really took the time to engage? Or even if you want to respond to everyone and be grateful, because you know you truly are, how thoroughly do you have to do it? Who 'makes the cut' because we've created this rather vicious cycle of validation for ourselves and each other?

There's the flipside too. How many meaningful conversations can you keep up at one time? Someone is bound to get upset if they don't get a satisfactory response. But isn't the emoji game a shell of a response? Like smiling at some or giving them a thumbs up and then not saying a word, the conversation ends there and you can move on quickly to the next?

I learned an interesting lesson when I started Girl Tribe. I was on a mission to acknowledge every comment. At one point, I was posting hearts under every comment thinking, *Yay, I've got this!* Then one day someone sent me a DM with kindly put constructive criticism (my favourite kind of criticism, to be honest). They suggested that perhaps it would be more meaningful if I wrote a proper response rather than posting hearts to everyone.

So, I changed.

I stopped commenting on everything. I got involved in conversations where I really had something to say and I tried my best to respond to those who did the same when I started a conversation. I know it's difficult to keep that up, but the next time you're setting up to scroll through someone's life for two hours, spend half of that time replying to your comments and see what a difference it makes. To you as a person, to the ones you acknowledged and, honestly, even to your algorithm! Everybody wins. Just like you would in life if you made an effort when someone tried to connect with you.

I have always admired my husband Nowshad, for one particular skill he has that I sorely lack: the ability to connect one-on-one with someone, even in the middle of a raging party. He remains deeply engaged, seldom distracted and is perfectly content having one or two meaningful conversations all night—unlike me, who's always bouncing around somewhat chaotically, always a little anxious that I should be in five places at the same time so I don't 'lose' anybody and unwittingly end up losing that moment itself. It's a terrible virtual habit I've adopted in real life too. One I desperately want to unlearn.

I know I keep comparing the real world with our virtual reality, but if I asked you to do an experiment with me, would you do it?

◎ Activity page

Circle the emojis you use most often.

♥

You must use these as a response through your day today with anyone you meet and no words.

List out all the things you do online that you do differently in real life.

Do you comment during someone else's argument? Interrupt a conversation?

Do you promote yourself on someone else's feed?

Do you walk up to someone you don't know and promote yourself?.

Do you ghost people aka walk away mid-conversation?

Do you ask everyone you meet 'Do you like me?' before you say anything else?

_____

_____

_____

_____

_____

_____

_____

_____

_____

_____

_____

_____

_____

Be honest and add anything else we haven't thought of. Drop me an Insta story so I can add it in the second print run of this book or, at the very least, repost it!

13

Kindness Is Key

> *'Unexpected kindness is the most powerful, least costly, and most underrated agent of human change.'*
> —Bob Kerrey

If you know me at all, then you know how deeply I value kindness and empathy. And chances are high that if we've ever met—or you've come across my social media—you've heard me speak passionately (and probably at length!) about the importance of it. I urge you now to pause for a moment and answer this question:

If I told you that the most valuable currency in in the world is Positivity and it comes in denominations of Kindness and Empathy, how much are you worth?

The best part is there is no barrier to entry here, you can be a 'positivity trillionaire' if you simply choose to. I jokingly refer to myself as Optimist Prime (a fun reimagining of Optimus Prime from the movie series, Transformers)—a wonderful moniker my dear friend Sid Shah gave me years ago and one I hold dearly because he himself has it in droves.

I personally feel positive people tend to be *kind*. Maybe because positive people have a happier outlook on life? But first, we should address what kind of happiness we are talking about. Hedonic happiness is all about yourself—increase pleasure, avoid pain—while eudemonic happiness includes others. Many great researchers like Keiko Otake, Satoshi Shimai, Junko Tanaka-Matsumi, Kanako Otsui and Barbara Fredrickson describe kindness as a combination of three things: the motivation to be kind to others, recognition of kindness in others and engaging in kind behaviour daily. What was the net finding? Happy people become more kind and grateful through the 'counting kindnesses intervention'.[89]

The counting kindnesses intervention asks people to become more aware of their own kind behaviour towards other people every day for one week. You simply must keep track of all the acts of kindness you perform through the week and report that daily number. You know you're going to love this one![90]

Counting Kindnesses Intervention

[⃝] Track your kindnesses through a week and share it with me on social media.

Mon	Tue	Wed	Thur	Fri	Sat	Sun

Having dug deep on this topic, I have been delighted to come across such exhaustive and extensive studies on happiness and kindness. I guess I'm not the only one obsessed with this topic. It isn't as 'fluffy' or 'soft' a pursuit as you might at first assume. Have you heard of the Subjective Happiness Scale?[91]

'The Subjective Happiness Scale seeks to conduct a global, subjective assessment of whether a person is happy or unhappy.

Response options: 7-point scale ranging from 1 to 7.

Total score: Responses to the four items are averaged, yielding a range from 1 to 7.'[92]

For each of the following statements and/or questions, please circle the point on the scale that you feel is most appropriate to you.

1. In general, I consider myself:

   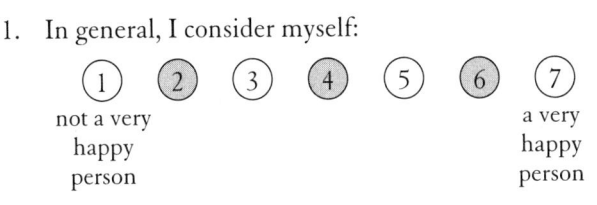

   not a very happy person — a very happy person

2. Compared with most of my peers, I consider myself:

   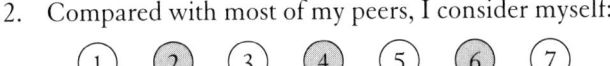

   less happy — more happy

3. Some people are generally very happy. They enjoy life regardless of what is going on, getting the most out of everything. To what extent does this characterization describe you?

   not at all — a great deal

4. Some people are generally not very happy. Although they are not depressed, they never seem as happy as they might be. To what extent does this characterization describe you?

   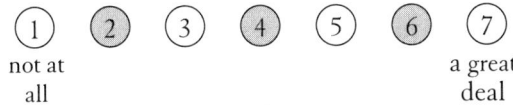

   not at all — a great deal

To score the scale, *reverse code the 4th item (i.e., turn a 7 into a 1, a 6 into a 2, a 5 into a 3, a 3 into a 5, a 2 into a 6, and a 1 into a 7), and compute the mean of the 4 items.

So, for example I answered as follows:

1. 6
2. 7
3. 5
4. 1

So, my final score is: 6+7+5+7* (because you reverse code the fourth item) and the average is 6.3.

Now you try it and share your results!

My Subjective Happiness Scale Score:

This is what your score means:

> The average score runs from about 4.5 to 5.5, depending on the group. College students tend to score lower (averaging a bit below 5) than working adults and older, retired people (who average 5.6). If you're past college age, and your happiness score is lower than 5.6, then you're less happy than the average person.[93]

If your score isn't up to where you want it to be, don't be sad. As I always say, without the bitter, the sweet ain't as sweet! And guess what? We have a wonderful fix for you!

No discussion on kindness is ever complete without the work of Hungarian-Canadian endocrinologist Hans Selye. He argues that to reduce the negative effects of everyday stressors, we need to do good for others. In his book, *The Stress of Life*, he suggests that in doing so our physiological responses to stress change[94]—which brings us to my favourite finding of all: the helper's high.

> ## Helper's High
>
> 'Helper's high' is another name for the uplifting feeling that you experience after doing a deed or act of kindness.
>
> This 'high' is rooted in our natural instincts to help our fellow humans. Evolution has wired us to help each other since helping others is benefical to human survival.
>
> Researchers discovered that helper's high is more than just a feeling. Biochemical analysis revealed that the high is accompanied by positive changes in the body's immune function and a lower level of stress hormones.
>
> Another way to describe the areas of the brain that release 'pain-relieving endorphins' is as the brain's pleasure centres.
>
> Endorphins are a group of opiate proteins, meaning they affect the brain like morphine.
>
> A study at the National Institute of Health showed that when people thought about giving money to a charity, the areas of the brain associated with pleasure lit up in the same way they light up when people thought about food or sex. A similar study at Emory University showed that helping others lit up the pleasure and reward part of one's brain.[89]

So now that you know that a sure-fire way to up your own happiness quotient is by engaging in an act of kindness for someone else, doesn't that make things a whole lot better and more promising? Let me connect this to social media for you. And I'll be brutally honest about how I got here.

There was a time where I would wake up in the morning and obsessively check my follower count, the number of likes on a post and how many comments I got. And then I would proceed to feel deeply gutted if the numbers didn't feel grand enough for the amount of effort or excitement I had poured into what I would posted. Then I would refresh and refresh and repeat the same process with another post till I was deeply immersed in a blue cloud of absence. The problem with access to 5.3 billion people on the internet[95] is that when you post something and nobody notices, you feel even more lonely than when you started. So, I did two things.

First, I turned off the public display of likes on my post and I turned off being able to see anyone else's either. So now I no longer judge a post by how many people double tapped it, I decide for myself if it engages me. Second, I made a rule for myself. The minute my eyes wander to the number of comments on a post, and I feel that little tinge of 'why didn't more people love this?', I immediately have to leave my page and visit someone else's and leave a meaningful comment. This generally elicits some kind of excitement back and I immediately feel good about myself, and I've given someone else a shot of dopamine too!

The great thing about the helper's high is that the more you give, the higher you get. And how much you give is always in your own hands. Isn't that so much more promising and rewarding that constantly worrying about who's coming to give you a pat on the back or double tap on your virtual face? I think so.

I found some fun facts for you on kindness too.

In an article by Sarah Tashjian, 'Does It Pay to Be Kind?', she identifies several benefits of kindness, all supported by scientific inquiry.[96] Here are some of them:

- Prosocial behaviours increase happiness and self-esteem
- Being kind improves how others see and accept you
- Kindness leads to reductions in risks for disease
- Neural networks related to reward fire when we're kind, and when we see others experience kindness

No two people express or behave with kindness the same way or to the same degree. Tashjian also identified that:

- People with less money show more generosity, charitability and helpfulness
- Children who are more social exhibit more prosocial behaviour
- Kindness is positively related to better self-regulation and less emotional reactivity[97]

Researchers from KindLab at Kindness.org conducted a meta-analysis of twenty-seven experimental studies. According to them, research supports that kindness has a significant effect on wellbeing.[98] KindLab also reported several other findings including:

- Kindness ranked above physical attractiveness in a potential mate.
- If a doctor expressed empathy and kindness, surveyed patients' colds shortened by one day

- Kindness can lower the effects of stress
- Being kind to others boosts psychological flourishing
- Kindness is an effective way to reduce state-level social anxiety

And here is why it is *so* important that we all dig deep and find our kindness: it is the kindness of strangers that will save us in the end, and wouldn't you like to be someone else's kind stranger? It's quite a magical feeling, trust me. To validate someone, to witness them, is the meaning of joy.

So now you're thinking, *Okay great, kindness is key, but is that really me?* Honestly, finding a scientifically validated list of what it takes to be a kind person doesn't really exist. What we do know from a variety of research is that there are a few recurring traits we find in kind people:[99]

- Empathy
- Good listening skills
- Social
- Generous
- Charitable
- Helpful
- Courteous
- Engages in perspective-taking

I am sure you've heard of random acts of kindness, I'm sure you've even engaged in some—whether it's giving up your seat in a crowded commuter train or helping someone carry a bag or letting them cut ahead of you in line. You don't always have to be saving someone from a burning car. Our brains tend to focus on the negative, scanning our environment for threats constantly.

But what if we spent more time identifying and immersing ourselves in all that is good?

During the pandemic, I stumbled upon *Some Good News* (2020), a digital show hosted by John Krasinski, dedicated entirely to reporting good news. I even started the India edition and I can tell you it kept me occupied and upbeat for much of the lockdown.

Loretta Graziano Breuning, author of *Meet Your Happy Chemicals*, contends that deep anxiety can result from following predominantly negative news. So, you have to feed your mind a healthy diet of good news just to stay alive. This hold true for the social media accounts you follow too.[100]

And, honestly, most good news is just bad news with a happy ending, which is why I choose to believe that it isn't over *till* things get better. And part of getting there is believing that we will.

I Don't Know Her Name, But I Got Her Digits

Don't be lazy and make judgements about people ... Ask about their stories. Listen. Be humble. Be open. Be teachable. Be a good neighbour.

—@marcandangel[101]

Something about this quote struck a chord with me. That's what we are, after all. We are all virtual neighbours. Unfortunately, we're often the loud, mean, unfriendly, encroaching ones. You know what, we probably didn't mean to but, somehow, we ended up dehumanizing each other, turning each other into a follower count.

But your followers are not robots; *they're people*. And it's time we treated them like that. These are people choosing to witness your life, experience your thoughts, get affected by your posts. What are you making them feel? I believe we would care more if we unsee the numbers and see the people.

I often tell people that the best way to make friends and connect with people is to ask someone about their life and genuinely listen to the answer. Have you ever noticed how people always ask you a question they themselves want to answer? Keep that in mind when they do. Always ask them back.

I know this is an old dilemma, but I spend a lot of time wondering why I am who I am. You know the cliché, 'I think therefore I am', right? *The Celestine Prophecy* by James Redfield (one of my favourite books) suggests that we as a race are becoming more aware of ourselves, which is also causing a fair amount of emotional anxiety because we're all wondering why we are here, unclear of the purpose of life. But at the same time, it is making us more empathetic.

> *When we dislike someone, or feel threatened by someone, the natural tendency is to focus on something we dislike about the person, something that irritates us. Unfortunately, when we do this—instead of seeing the deeper beauty of the person and giving them energy—we take energy away and actually do them harm. All they know is that they suddenly feel less beautiful and less confident, and it is because we sapped their energy.*
>
> —James Redfield, *The Celestine Prophecy*

The point is, I live my life with everything from my point of view. I walk around living with myself, in my head 24/7, just as you do. But you are the hero of your story, and I am just the supporting cast.

The War of the (Virtual) Worlds

A few years ago, there was a massive YouTube vs TikTok war that exploded on the internet. The case against TikTokers was 'cringeworthy' content, the case against YouTubers was jealousy and internal discontent. I watched the controversy with a heavy heart. All I want to say is that this was not the purpose of social media. These platforms were created to express our creativity, connect with people and possibly to feel less alone in the world. Hence, 'social' media. What no one realized was that we were slowly but surely creating another kind of social classism. This time, virtually.

It never ceases to amaze me how that happens. We're all the same but we're so busy trying to prove we're different. Anyway, the videos were flagged and removed and the rage eventually subsided, but I definitely learned a few things. The first was that for every angry ranter, there is a voice of reason that expresses itself with clarity and kindness. I was really impressed with how TikToker Nitish Rajput explained the problem and urged people not to make it about the platform but rather the *people* who should be held accountable.[102] I also liked how YouTuber Prajakta Koli found a silver lining in the whole thing by saying she was happy to see that in the whole furore, what came to light was that people are genuinely outraged by violence and hatred and were quick to report it.[103] It certainly gives me hope that, while we're building a virtual society, we're also grooming its young representatives. Those who will guide Generation Apha into a kinder, cleaner virtual reality.

We all know that there's been a lot of questionable content across various platforms over the years, and I believe these platforms must be vigilant and take appropriate action when something is flagged. But, at the end of the day, it is on us, as people, to not invent a new kind of virtual classism.

I believe we can get past this with empathy and kindness. But it is important that, as creators and consumers, we focus on making and watching positive content instead of letting negativity cloud our mind space. It is never okay to propagate hate, violence, gender inequality, racism, bigotry or any other form of hatred. In fact, if you come across it, you must report it. We can all be part of the solution together.

This isn't a war of the platforms, this is a virtual society that needs to check its behaviour. People are already suffering so much right now. As creators, we must use our voices and platforms responsibly, spread positivity and stand together. It really should not matter what social media you're on. What matters is that you have your heart in the right place.

It's Not You, It's the Algorithm

Most creators have a deep love–hate relationship with social media algorithms. I think it's important I spend some time on this. First up, what does a social media algorithm really do?

Sprout Social has explained how Instagram algorithm's ranking is based on the following signals:[104]

- **Interest:** Your likely interest in content is based on engagement with similar topics.

- **Timeliness:** More recent posts are prioritized over older ones.
- **Relationship:** Content from accounts you've interacted with more is prioritized.
- **Frequency:** How often you use Instagram factors into what the top posts in your feed will be.
- **Following:** How many people you follow affects what you see—you may see less content from any one account if you follow a lot of accounts.
- **Usage:** Spending more time on the app scrolling through your Instagram feed means you'll see more or even everything the algorithm has to offer you at the moment.

Simply put, it applies a set of rules and signals that rank the content on social media based on how likely it is that people will like it and interact with it. Why do we need them? Because for users who follow hundreds or thousands of accounts it does the job of sifting through the mass of content and deciding what you would most like to see. In theory, that is. There's also the belief that social media algorithms exist purely to push branded content that wouldn't perform well organically but that's what pays the platform's bills, so it gets VIP treatment for a suitable fee. But here is what I have learned about social media algorithms:

1. **It is ever-changing. On purpose.** The thing about Instagram, for example, is that it makes money from advertising. So, the app wants you to stay plugged in for as long as possible, so that you can be shown more ads. That's why the algorithm is designed to show you the content you like the most. If you're entertained, you'll stay on Instagram longer. Every change the algorithm makes is designed to

refine that exact same process. They just want to show you content that you'll engage with. And that brings us to how the algorithm decides whether your content should be shown or not.

2. **The formula is very simple.** The more engagement your content gets, the more you are considered relevant and engaging. So, your content will be shown to those with similar interests to yours. There is no secret ingredient. Just create engaging content that is relevant to your audience and let your people find you.

3. **Social media is about being social.** Ask yourself, does your content spark a conversation? 'As a simple rule-of-thumb to follow, look at your content before posting it. If it doesn't encourage people to be social, then it shouldn't be on social media.'[105]

4. **Follow the 80/20 Rule.** Eighty per cent of your content should be entertaining or of some value to your audience and twenty per cent should be about you and your personal flexes or your brand.

5. **Quality control.** The first rule of thumb: as yourself, 'Would I read/watch this?' Second rule: 'Would I send this to anyone?' After you create your content, run this quick exercise. Try to think of ten different comments people might leave. If those ten came easily to you then that's probably an engaging piece of content; if not, you're probably better off editing or ditching the content.

6. **Interact back.** Notice how often you reply to your comments with a conversation-ending reply. A random heart or thank you generally puts a bow on things right there. How often do you ask a follow-up question and really engage? I'll be honest, I personally struggle with this a lot myself because

of the sheer volume of comments, but I'm trying to be more present in my responses as well. Sometimes, less with more meaning is just more valuable overall.

Social Media Rehab

I decided to do an experiment to consciously document my social media activity for an entire week. I think the results were pretty eye-opening. Perhaps you would like to try it too.

What I did this week online

	Mon	Tue	Wed	Thur	Fri	Sat	Sun
How many times I opened Instagram.	11	12	16	14	13	7	10
How many people I interacted with in a meaningful way online.	4	3	6	4	4	2	4

According to the *Journal of Social and Clinical Psychology*:

> It is recommended to use social media for thirty minutes per day for better physical and mental health. The study also suggests that it is better to distribute your time between three apps, so that you can maintain engagement

and not lose out. Those who maintained balance reported lower levels of anxiety, depression and stress. What's more, neither did they experience FoMO. All in all, the less time you spend on social media, the less you will face self-confidence and mental health issues.[106]

Now here's the scary stats part. In India, we spend at least a third of our waking hours on our mobiles. The average hours spent on a mobile per day per user surged by around 4.5 per cent from 3.7 hours in 2019 to 4.7 hours in 2021. Indians spent 655 billion hours on mobiles in 2021, a 37 per cent increase since 2019 (381 billion hours).[107]

According to Nielsen, 'nearly thirty million Indians who are online are members of social networking sites and about two-thirds of them spend time on these social networking sites daily. More importantly, Indians spend more time on social media than they do using personal email.'[108]

You know what happens here next.

How much time do you spend online?

	Mon	Tue	Wed	Thur	Fri	Sat	Sun
Total time on Instagram							
How many YouTube videos I watched							

Reality Bites

> *Life imitates art and art imitates life until both imitate imitation—reality TV.*
>
> —Brian Spellman

I am a self-confessed social media and reality TV addict, and I scour OTT platforms for shows that provide a heady mix of both. Perhaps I'm looking for answers or just for other people with the same questions? I have a few favourite shows that have touched upon the social (media) dilemma with equal parts gravitas and humour. I even reached out to some of the shows' contestants to understand how it changed or evolved their personal understanding of the game, if at all. If you're into unpacking virtual reality I highly recommend you dig deep into your OTT archives and binge these asap: *Black Mirror*, which unpacks technology in the most bone-chilling way. In *Upload*, it is 2033 and humans can literally 'upload' themselves into a virtual afterlife. The protagonist explores the pros and cons of 'digital heaven' while bonding with his living customer service representative, who's struggling with the pressures of her job. *The Social Dilemma* is a seriously sobering documentary that lays bare how social media is designed to nurture addiction to maximize profit with the less than savoury side effects of manipulating people's views, emotions and behaviour while spreading conspiracy theories and disinformation. Fun!

Catfish is a great documentary about catfishing, that is, posing as someone else to elicit their attention, and how the documentary-makers themselves get caught in this tumultuous web only to get an MTV reality show out of it. So I suppose things turned out okay.

The Circle (2017) is a reality game show where contestants try to become 'influencers' to win prize money. I even asked our favourite desi boy contestant Shubham Goel about his experience and this is what he had to say, 'My views on social media have evolved since going on *The Circle*! After building incredible friendships through *The Circle*, I have grown to see some benefits with social media including building friendships, expressing yourself, and creating a community! I still see some cons in social media aka Social Medusa including the mental health addiction with it, the false sense of reality, and the constant comparison contest that social media puts all through!'

Probably still one of my favourites back from 2017 is *Ingrid Goes West*. A mentally unstable young woman crashes the wedding of an Instagram influencer she feels she has a personal relationship with because the influencer once commented on one of her pictures.

I also have a deep love for podcasts like *Love Unplugged*, *This American Life* and *Serial*—my list is literally endless. DM me and I'll hit you up with an algorithm-free recommendation if you tell me what you're looking for.

The point is that art very much imitates life and by the time this book hits the market there will be dozens more shows, movies and podcasts to rave about. What I do suggest though, is that you dig deep and learn as much as you can about your own social behaviour from the characters you most resonate with.

14

A Word on Positive Masculinity

> *Empowering women isn't just the right thing to do. It is the smart thing to do.*
> —Barack Obama

I want to take a moment here to appreciate all the men who have joined the conversation since we kicked off the #ignorenomoreonline campaign, not just by verbalizing their support but actively reporting and confronting perpetrators. I firmly believe that men are the most impactful role models for other men. If they join the conversation we will make so much more progress so much faster.

To this end, I asked Nowshad Rizwanullah (Cofounder CEO of MissMalini Entertainment, Cofounder of Good Creator Co and CEO of my heart!) to share his views and experience, especially after participating in two digital social experiments we conducted on a few good men. In the first experiment, we asked all the guys in the video to answer the sexist questions we often come across as women online and offline and in the second we asked them to read aloud some of the oh-so-creepy DMs women are subjected to on an almost daily basis—from the guy talking to himself in my DMs to a vast array of dick pics. Here are Nowshad's unfiltered thoughts on the matter!

Nowshad Rizwanullah says ...

As Malini's life and business partner over the last fifteen years, I'm not surprised she felt the need to write an entire book on behaving better online. Malini's digital immersion—and the fame that has accompanied it—has exposed her to some of the best and worst impulses found on social media. For every positive, uplifting comment left by a fan, there often lurks an equally disturbing, generally salacious contribution by another. Sadly, almost all of the time the filth is contributed by a male profile.

It doesn't take someone of Malini's stature to fall prey to this abuse. Several years ago, we asked some of our female colleagues to compile a selection of recent unsolicited messages they had received in their DMs. Next, we invited a group of unsuspecting men to read these out loud on camera. What started out as a laugh very quickly devolved into a stomach-churning onslaught of hypersexualized attacks. Almost every message culminated in crass and explicit sexual fantasies, laced with profanities, threats of violence, and a perverse macho entitlement to being a jerk.

Surely we can do better than this. The internet can be an empowering, exhilarating place, thanks to its open access, tools for self-expression, and the power to connect with anyone, anywhere, anytime. Yet these very same qualities are being abused to the point where women no longer feel safe just scrolling their feeds anymore.

When we started MissMalini, one of our driving motivations was to give voice to young Indians, and to celebrate the dynamism and energy of a new generation that was until then inadequately and inaccurately represented in legacy media. We took a conscious decision to celebrate the positive rather than prey on the negative, because how you make other people feel matters. If we want to live in a less negative world, someone needs to re-balance our attention towards the power of the positive. The results were impressive. The more positive our coverage became, the more positive our user comments trended. MissMalini became known as a place that put a smile on your face; where it was the norm to say nice things about the celebrities we follow, not the exception.

When I was asked to share my thoughts on the topic of toxic masculinity, it was quite daunting to think of something profound to say, or to come up with new ideas that could create a dent in an issue as pervasive as online trolling and harassment. It occurred to me that this is where many of us probably get stuck, in feeling helpless and hopeless against a problem we recognize but feel powerless to change. Drawing a lesson from our experience with positive media, I realized that it doesn't take much to start making a difference, and it's not so much about combating 'toxic masculinity' as it is about promoting 'positive masculinity' (you'll forgive me for not debating these loaded terms here for the sake or brevity).

Let me share two simple but illustrative examples of how easy it can be to have a positive impact.

There are two short sentences totalling less than ten words that have unwittingly earned me the greatest amount of praise as a proponent of positive masculinity: 'CEO & Mr to @MissMalini. I'm OK with that.' What I thought was just a clever Instagram bio turned out to mean much more to the many women who have gone out of their way to thank me for it over the years; symbolic of a man unintimidated with his wife's success, comfortable with his role in her journey and unafraid to admit out loud that she's way, way more talented than he is. A small gesture that nonetheless made a big impact.

Another example comes in the form of a question a lot of men (and some women) ask me: what is it like working with your wife? I do understand that general intrigue around marriage dynamics can drive this curiosity—but I've never heard Malini being asked what it's like working with her husband. When I started pointing out this asymmetry to the men who ask me the question, I was surprised by how enlightening this simple observation could be. Many didn't realize they were falling back on deep-seated stereotypes and dated gender norms—but they immediately acknowledged the fallacy once pointed out. Did I change the world? Maybe not. But I'm pretty sure I gave some well-intentioned people something to think about. Sometimes you just need to take a conscious moment to speak up and offer a better perspective.

I'm obviously not suggesting that updating your Instagram bio and being a more thoughtful conversationalist is going to solve all of society's problems. But maybe it's time we are all more conscious of the impact our words and actions can make, both positive and negative. Maybe we can all make an extra effort to project the kind of digital society we'd be proud to populate. Maybe the content we produce or consume can take more responsibility in the way it shapes our feelings and our discourse.

And maybe, just maybe, we can all read Malini's book, embrace its lessons, and embody the example of the Queen of Positivity herself. 😊

I have to share a funny (ongoing) dilemma I face on social media being married to someone who revels in JoMO (the joy of missing out), not FoMO. I have picked way too many fights with him over seemingly stupid stuff like 'Why didn't you wish me happy birthday on Instagram?' or 'How come you never comment on my posts?' These are half-joking arguments but let me admit—only half. I genuinely went through a phase of feeling virtually rejected by my husband not celebrating every milestone with me on social media and tried to tell myself it's not about the validation but authenticity of it all. Over the years, I have come to understand that he is just wired differently and when he does put up a post or comment on a picture (usually of our dog), it brings me joy. The same kind I felt all those years ago when I knew a friend was tuned in to my show on the radio. But I don't take it personally when he doesn't and, for his part, he religiously double taps at least three of my pictures whenever he does log on to social media. We have achieved a comfortable understanding and, more than anything else (as Che Kurien, editor of *GQ India*, succinctly pointed out while kindly reviewing my book), every influencer needs a 'Rizwan' aka a Nowshad to keep them grounded and probably even sane. I am deeply grateful and so lucky to have found mine.

I <3 you @nrizwanu and it doesn't matter how many times you double tap my pictures, you're my IRL double tap for life!

MALINI'S INTERNET RULE # 3

Spark joy (with your next post)

15

Women, Community and the Internet: Malini's Girl Tribe

> *When women support each other, incredible things happen.*
> —Unknown

Hopefully by now you know a little bit about Malini's Girl Tribe. If not, here's its simple premise.

Malini's Girl Tribe is an attempt to make the internet a safer, kinder, more constructive place for women. It exists as a community on Facebook called Malini's Girl Tribe, on Instagram as @malinisgirltribe and we also have our very own free app, also called Malini's Girl Tribe. But these are just the tools we use to connect with each other. The true heart of the tribe is in the fact that this sisterhood exists on the three pillars of empathy, kindness and positivity.

We have crossed over from virtual to reality with a physical community aspect as well and I have found solid proof here that, given the right guidance and a gentle nudge of positive reinforcement, we can truly learn how to use the internet in a whole different way. One that is satisfying, rewarding and just a happy experience!

With over 1,00,000 active women (15x more engaged and likely to respond to a conversation with a coherent, in-depth response than people are on public Facebook profiles we see about 200 comments every 12 minutes). Meaningful ones at that! The best part? You don't have to be a celebrity or an 'influencer' to expect a response or any kind of acknowledgement. You just have to be you and be kind. This is the kind of currency in which we have the ability to be supremely wealthy with very little effort.

There is ample proof in the way the tribe works—it's in its very DNA—that it is possible to unlearn caustic online behaviour, that social media can be a beautiful, bonding experience between complete strangers, even across borders, and that people can learn basic netiquette and self-correct as a collective if they are veering off-course.

And today, it allows me to point out a startling difference in social behaviour. My public Instagram elicits a whole variety of response-types from zero f*cks given to just bizarre bot behaviour. Like, someone explain this to me please; it was a response to questions I had posted:

lukymakry Thank you Maam @pokus_pounds_crypto I have so much joy ever since you helped me Sir I have made over $20,000 with your help and strategies I promise to bring more people who need to recover their lose @pokus_pounds_crypto

The questions were: Why do you use social media; what purpose does it serve in your life? What is one thing that you now know about social media/the internet that you wish someone had told you before you joined? If you could change one thing about the internet, what would that be?

When I posted the *exact same* questions in the group, I got hundreds of extremely lucid and well-articulated answers.

I found the answers fascinating. I've shared the most common and insightful ones below. Please take a minute to reflect, and fill out your own answers in the table below.

ⓘ 1. Why do you use social media? What purpose does it serve in your life?	2. What is one thing that you now know about social media/the internet that you wish someone had told you before you joined?	3. If you could change one thing about the internet, what would that be?

Unsee the Numbers and See the People

You may think this is because of the demographic of the group but I beg to differ. I feel it is the *intent* of the group. It is the understanding that within this group there is a society, and a society has its rules—or a code of conduct, if you will. On social media, on the other hand, there's no governance, making it a free-for-all. It's like stepping into the worst part of the Mad Max trilogy, where it's survival of the sharpest tongue and death by oblivion.

And finally, the most important reason why there's no hate on this group is because you are *seen*. You have a witness—thousands, in fact. You have been accepted as a member of the community, so you are given the respect we often struggle to command in a virtual world without order. It all goes back to finding a witness to your life and evoking enough feeling in the other person that they care about what you think, or at the very least, they care that you exist. The only way we can do that is if we unsee the numbers and see the people. *That* is what will evoke any kind of empathy and kindness. You'll care if you know who Anjali is; you won't if she's just follower number 247.

There is a James Bond short story that talks about the law of the quantum of solace, which I believe is a very poignant explanation for what has happened here.

> The governor character in the Ian Fleming [...] defines it as 'a precise figure defining the comfort, humanity, and fellow feeling required between two people for love to survive. If the quantum of solace is 0, then love is dead.' He then introduces the law of the quantum of solace as follows: 'I've seen flagrant infidelities patched up, I've seen crimes, and even murder foreign by the other party, let alone bankruptcy, and other forms of social crime. Incurable disease, blindness, disaster, all of these can be overcome. But never the death of common humanity in one of the partners. I've thought about this, and I've invented a rather high-sounding title for this basic factor in human relations. I have called it the law of the quantum of solace.' In the same story, James Bond

> comments on the law of the quantum of solace as follows: 'That's a splendid name for it. It's certainly impressive enough, and of course I see what you mean. I should say you're absolutely right. Quantum of solace, the amount of comfort. Yes, I suppose you can say that all love and friendship is based in the end on that. Human beings are very insecure. When the other person not only makes you feel insecure, but actually seems to want to destroy you, it's obviously the end. The quantum of solace stands at zero. You've got to get away to save yourself.'[109]

So, in my assessment of the virtual world, we somehow ended up with our quantum of solace at zero, and that's when everything went to sh*t. But don't despair, I believe there is hope! If we can somehow generate empathy and kindness in a group from nothing, made up of the same people that live on Instagram or TikTok, it's only a matter of social conditioning. People will do what they see everyone else doing. The key is to unlearn whatever we taught ourselves about social media and start from scratch.

I stumbled across an Instagram live video during quarantine—you know how it goes, you watch for a few seconds, drop a comment, someone says hi, perhaps you move on. But I chanced upon a conversation the Keshav Suri Foundation was having with poet and podcaster Josh Rivers. He does a segment called Homo Poetry, a fun little spin, I suppose, of being locked down, being gay and loving poetry. I love it! He said something that really caught my attention. He read a poem about lies and then went on to explain that of course: 'There are enough times I can be honest with myself, with you and live my truth, but sometimes, I want to make the world something you deserve to live in and you can't always do that with the truth.'[110]

Damn, that's deep. And hello, that's social media! But what if we could? What if we *could* make the world something we deserve to live in by telling the truth? What would that take?

16

Sparking Joy Online

> *Believe what your heart tells you when you ask, 'Does this spark joy?'*
> —Marie Kondo

I borrowed the title of this chapter from the Netflix show *Tidying Up with Marie Kondo* (2019). She says only hold on to the things that 'spark joy' and let the rest go. Perhaps we should apply the same principle to the things we offer others. *Especially on social media.*

When my first book was published, I realized that I could spark joy too. My book was called *#ToTheMoon: How I Blogged My Way to Bollywood* but it turns out that the book wasn't about Bollywood at all. It was a story of hopes and dreams. About a girl born in the small town of Allahabad who had this whirlwind ride and ended up following her dreams to Mumbai. I can say without a shadow of a doubt that I am a living, breathing example that the Bombay Dream is real. And you don't have to have a ton of money, a godfather or make any compromises you're not comfortable with to make your dreams come true. All you need is hard work, passion and FoMO!

I went on my book tour and met so many young girls who told me that the book inspired them to follow their dreams. How amazing is that? That's when it hit me how much of what we put out into the universe—as simple as it may seem to us—can have a huge impact on those who witness it. Especially through something as frequently used as our social media.

For the longest time I couldn't figure out who I was. I'm not Huda Beauty or Kim Kardashian or a Bollywood star. So, who is Malini?

In writing this book I've been processing a lot of my own feelings about social media and how hard it is to keep up with the race. I realized that somehow when I went to the Girl Tribe my eyes didn't wander to the likes. I cared more about what people were saying to each other rather than the numbers. I love the honest questions we are asking and the answers we are sharing ... It is an experience like no other, honestly, and it makes me feel more confident, secure and, frankly, relevant. Because in this new world of creators, performers and social media stars, I feel a bit lost sometimes. I am very happy and proud to have been part of the first digital wave and I am so happy that hundreds and thousands of young influencers have found a voice and the ability to follow their dreams just by being themselves—it is absolutely incredible, and I am so very proud to have had some role to play in it. But some days it's hard to keep running. Some days I just want to sit down and not feel the urge to compete or compare. Some days I want to feel as proud of having had five meaningful exchanges than getting 10,000 likes. But I don't always know if that's okay—if I stop running, will the world just pass me by? So maybe I'll jog for a while so things don't zip by so quickly any more. Maybe I'll jog and you'll jog with me.

Btw, I think this realization came from accepting my insecurities and some jealousy (yes, that was why I was listening to the Pet Shop Boys on repeat). Not all green-eyed monsters are about romance.

> *At dead of night, when strangers roam*
> *The streets in search of anyone who'll take them home*
> *I lie alone, the clock strikes three*
> *And anyone who wanted to could contact me*
> *At dead of night, 'till break of day*
> *Endless thoughts and questions keep me awake*
> *It's much too late*
> *Where've you been?*

Who've you seen?
You didn't phone when you said you would!
Do you lie?
Do you try
To keep in touch? You know you could
I've tried to see your point of view
But could not hear or see
For jealousy
I never knew time pass so slow
I wish I'd never met you, or that I could bear to let you go
—Pet Shop Boys, 'Jealousy'

More than anything, I hate feeling envious of my friends. I don't ever want to be that person and I don't think I am but this greed for social (media) currency was starting to make me go *Black Swan* a little, LOL. So enough. I don't need Instagram to hide my hearts away, I need my mind to reprogramme what it defines to be loved.

And so, I realized I am happiest being Optimist Prime! I'm making that a thing! And the only way to do that honestly is to slay the green-eyed monster and all the negativity it brings.

There is a beautiful scene in the movie *Inside Out* where Bing Bong is struggling with his feelings and Joy isn't able to help him, Sadness is. Because sometimes it's okay to not be okay. But it's never good to pretend you are okay, okay?!

Sadness: I'm sorry they took your rocket. They took something you loved.
Bing Bong: It's gone. Forever.
Joy: Sadness! Don't make him feel worse!
Sadness: [to Joy] Sorry.

Bing Bong: It's all I had left of Riley.
Sadness: I bet you and Riley had great adventures.
Bing Bong: [choking up] Oh, they were wonderful. Once we flew back in time. We had breakfast twice that day.
Joy: [annoyed]Sadness!
Sadness: It sounds amazing. I bet Riley liked it.
Bing Bong: She did. We were best friends.
Sadness: Yeah. It's sad.
[Bing Bong hugs Sadness tightly and sobs]
Bing Bong: I'm okay now. Come on. The train station is this way.

—Inside Out

You may not have realized this but your social media identity is a digital representative of who you are. And it's leaving an everlasting imprint. So, make it a good one.

So now you're thinking, *Shoot! My imprint has a few muddy footprints. How do I erase them?* The truth is, you can't but you can do better—starting *now*. Literally from your next tweet or comment. You can be your best self. You might also be thinking, *Fine, that applies to trolling but what if I was justified to troll? What if someone said something that made me look bad/feel bad and I'm just standing up for myself?* I'm not saying let people walk all over you but there's no need to do any sort of public justification unless you want people to watch the show.

And again, I'm only telling you this because I know I got it wrong on more than one occasion.

Here's what happened. I was doing interviews on the International Indian Film Academy Awards (IIFA) red carpet. There was a singer who got upset with me because I didn't interview her when I was interviewing actors on the red carpet.

She tweeted about it and I thought if I tweeted back explaining myself nicely, she'd let it go. But it only upset her more.

So, I had this conversation on Twitter. All the while thinking I was doing the right thing.

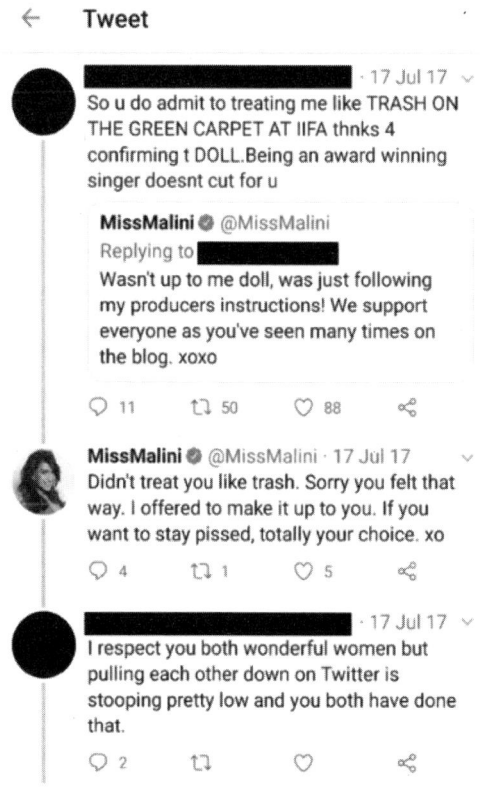

And then I saw this tweet. They weren't trolling me. It was simply expressing genuine disappointment about both of us.

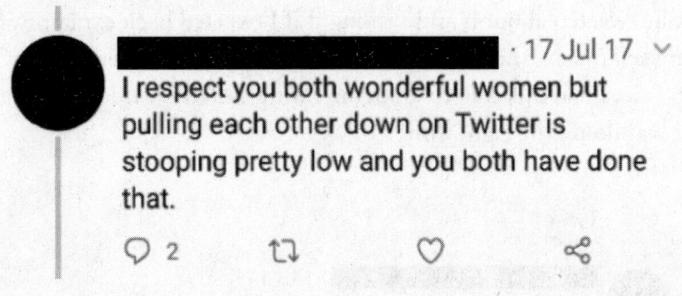

It made me step back and take a pause and think, okay wait, if this was the real world, how differently would I have approached this?

Would I have called everyone over, saying, 'Hey I'm not wrong but I'm still saying sorry, come see.' Or would I have tried to sort it out with her one-on-one? I realized the truth is if you're sorry, you're unconditionally sorry. Or you're not really sorry. You're just embarrassed.

I have learnt that it is okay to make mistakes. But it is not okay to refuse to learn from them.

SPEECH FILTERS
THINK BEFORE SPEAKING

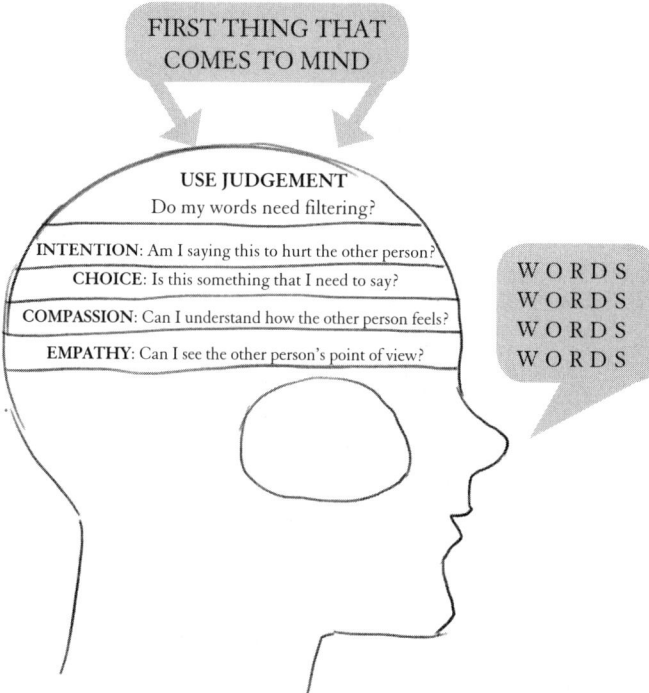

I once had a great conversation with this absolute sunshine of a girl called Mansha on a podcast. It was so comfortable and engaging (largely due to her insightful questions) that I found myself wanting to quote *myself* from some of the things I said myself! I know that sounds really silly but sometimes you have such clarity of thought in a moment, it pours out of you in the exact way you've always wanted. And more often than not that happens without warning. Serendipity, they call it, right? Maybe I'm also finding the right words in the process of figuring myself out.

So, in case any aspiring writers are reading this book, I have learnt a golden lesson in writing mine. When you're stuck, read a book, listen to a podcast, call a friend and strike up a conversation and more often than not you'll strike a match and fire up the cosy fireplace inside your ... never mind, that was a failed analogy. I'd rather not belabour the point, but you know what I mean! (I don't advise binge-watching anything, it has not so far achieved the same effect, but maybe I'm watching the wrong things—I'm looking at you *Too Hot to Handle*. Anyway, I digress. Since I found myself (LOL) so inspiring in this podcast, give it a listen if you like?

What Are Your Reflections in the Black Mirror?

Truly the 'future' we talk about is here and we are all adjusting with how to live with this kind of information overload as well as our security and having all our data exposed. Perhaps there are some parallels since the show does mimic real life almost eerily.

Also, did you know why the show is called *Black Mirror*? Because when your phone is not in use it looks like a black mirror! Blew my mind when Ankit aka *Gadgetwala* told me that!

I feel like I deeply resonate with the meme 'this meeting could have been an email' or 'me watching my phone waiting for it to stop ringing so I can say what's up on text instead'. I mean, I think of myself as a social person, I, in fact, *love* people—so then what is preventing me from having a one-on-one interaction with them? Don't worry, you're not alone. Here's why we all do it.

1. It feels more private. Anyone can overhear your phone call. Texting is a little more secure and secretive. Especially when you want to communicate something in a room full of people to just one. Plus, you can easily tap out a text than find a secluded conference room in a work environment.
2. It's less time consuming. It just *feels* less demanding than a phone call because the recipient can choose to respond when they feel like, and you can do away with all the 'niceties' and five minutes of small talk and dive right into the purpose of the conversation.
3. Probably the most important part for me is it's easier to multitask. Same feels for Zoom meetings with the cameras off. Being on the phone can be daunting; I can text, talk, eat lunch and plan my wardrobe for tomorrow all at the same time if I have the freedom to respond at my pace and have the luxury of not paying attention the first time I skim the text. It allows me to continue my hectic schedule without missing a beat.

And while I justify all of this to myself, I realize why I struggle so much with social media fatigue or even just screen fatigue. Because (and here's another meme to go with that thought): my workday sometimes feels like a series of emails/texts I'm dying to get done with just so I can watch Netflix! (The other screen we're doom scrolling when we're not busy overthinking all the likes we didn't get!)

The other thing that's really been getting to me lately is having to live once, and relive for Instagram a second time. Because everything I do gets documented on my social media, I may find myself admiring a beautiful view while stressing about how well I've captured it for the gram while still deeply conflicted about missing it! Then there's the whole 'real time' posting dilemma. Does my social feed need to be real time? Then where do I make room for 'me time'? I kid you not, I've found myself cancelling plans and staying home in PJs doing nothing *just* so my Instagram can catch up with my real life.

~~~

Tell me I'm not alone and share a post with me where you either weren't fully present or were deeply aware that you're doing it for the gram on some level.

17

What's the Tea?

> *To write a letter is to send a message to the future; to speak of the present with an addressee who is not there, knowing nothing about how that person is (in what spirits, with whom) while we write and, above all, later: while reading over what we have written. Correspondence is the utopian form of conversation because it annihilates the present and turns the future into the only possible place for dialogue.*
> —Ricardo Piglia, *Respiración Artificial*

I love a good crossover or Easter egg in a book or movie (much like Stephen King does in his novels), so here is mine. In my first book I wrote a letter to my eighteen-year-old self. In this one, I'm writing one to yours.

Dear Gen Z and Alpha,

This one's from me to you because it's possible you picked up this book hoping to unlock the secrets to social media stardom. You're not wrong, but I'm going to be honest with you and tell you that it all comes at a price.

If you're wondering why I avoided talking about the pandemic in detail so far, I am here to tell you it was a conscious decision. I started writing this book back in 2019, believe it or not, so when Covid hit, nothing in my wildest nightmares could have predicted how long it was planning to stay. And I struggled with how much it would change this book. But the truth is, if anything, it only made everything I believe we need to fix about our virtual existence so much more pressing. I have left below my original epilogue (which I wrote in 2020—just 133 days into lockdown), where you can clearly see the shock and horror were just about settling in.

2 August 2020: So here's a chapter I wasn't expecting to write at all. Chances are, if I had stuck to schedule, my book would be out by now, completely oblivious to how the world had so irreversibly changed while it was in fittings. I have been watching this pandemic unfold with equal parts shock, awe and horror—and more than a little disbelief. Fluctuating wildly between 'it can't be as bad as they're making it sound' and 'I really hope this isn't how it all ends' (We have so much left to do, including submitting this manuscript!). And then it struck me. Aside from being such an unprecedented occurrence in our lifetimes, the entire *way* we are receiving and processing information today is right out of an episode of *Black Mirror*. From fifteen-second #Covid19 TikTok trends, to Netflix clips about Korean dramas that predicted this outbreak two years ago, to countless hilarious coronavirus memes.

There is an absolutely endless stream of information pouring into our minds. What is particularly striking is that given that this is a global experience—today, every podcast, every late night host, every news outlet and every single celebrity and influencer is talking about a shared experience. And they're doing it on social media. So let's unpack this a little bit.

In 1912, when we last witnessed a pandemic of epic proportions, there was obviously no internet, there was also no TV or radio stations. News was confined to local newspapers. Today, we're sharing 2.5 quintillion bytes (which is 1,000 quadrillions, which is 1,000 trillions) of data day *each day* to about three billion people (almost half the world's population).

Maybe that's why this doesn't feel real. Because my WiFi is still working. And if the WiFi is working, it means the world must be 'okay'. Because thanks to my modern-day conditioning and sensibilities (aka Hollywood), death, disease and plague-like devastation doesn't happen where the lights are on. You only know you're in trouble when the TV turns to white noise, the radio crackles to a halt and the lights flicker to darkness. Not while 200 million troops are currently deployed in battle on PUBG!

As I type this I realize how insane that logic sounds, but I kid you not, my brain has been struggling to make sense of it all. How can we be in the middle of a global pandemic while binge watching *Money Heist* (2017) and swipe through Instagram Lives? But the truth is, we are. We are well and truly in the 'future' we always talked about. The only difference being that we expected to have flying cars and orange hair and little eye gadgets that changed your makeup for you with one click (thank you *The Fifth Element* (1997), for those expectations) but instead we have the very odd paradox of twenty-first century unlimited access to information at the speed of light but the same set of lungs we had back in 1912 to breathe with.

This chapter may be highly redundant by the time you read this book, but as a turning point in my lifetime, I feel like I should document the role social media has had to play. Perhaps when we tally up the scores we'll have learnt

> something about ourselves and the application of technology to literally save heads and heart.
>
> Considering we are now on Day 133 of lockdown in Mumbai, I suppose it's safe to say we're not going to forget this happened any time soon. Books will be written, movies will be made, vaccines will be tested and memes will flood our feeds. But as we battle one global pandemic on the ground, the other one that rages on is the troll pandemic online and we haven't even considered making a vaccine or some 'social distancing' rules for it. We haven't even declared it an emergency. And that begs the question: Who's in change here? Like, who is the internet police? Who's looking out for the health of our virtual society? Essentially, who you gonna call? Ghost Busters? The WHO (World Health Organization)? Who? And I guess more importantly, what will you say?
>
> 'Hello 100? The internet is broken. Can somebody please hit CTRL + ALT + DEL?'

LOL, oh how naive to be so fed up so quickly! It all seems like such a distant memory already. Horrifying, but is it over? I guess the good news is I lived to tell the tell the tale or, in this case, write the book ...

The internet has given me my entire career and every incredible opportunity in life, but it has undoubtedly taken its pound of flesh in return.

I'm not saying this to scare you off or discourage you, I just want you to know that virtual reality, not unlike the real world, has its equal manifestations of heaven and hell. You are the main character of this saga. It is now entirely up to you how to navigate that. Decide whether you want to look at your life as a fun-filled rom-com with some sad but funny and glossy bits or a lonely end-of-the-world kinda horror show where everyone's turning into zombies, and proceed accordingly. In his book, *Humankind: A Hopeful History*, Rutger Bregman shares a great insight: 'the mechanism that makes us the kindest species also makes us the cruellest species on the planet. People are social animals, but we have a fatal flaw: we feel more affinity for those who are most like us [...] So what is this radical idea? That most people, deep down, are pretty decent.'[111] I love that he quotes the old greats like Anton Chekhov, 'Man will become better when you show him what he is like.' So let me do just that. Let me hold up a mirror (selfie) to you, my dear Gen Z and Alpha.

You live in a time where you can make *anything* your career. In fact, in your lifetime there will be careers that do not yet exist. Perhaps you could be an usher on Elon Musk's tourist rocket bus to the moon (imagine that Instagram flex!). Today, you can be a stylist's assistant, a content creator, a makeup artist, an NFT designer or blockchain coder. You can take anything you love to do and get paid to do it. Your ikigai is there for the taking.

So tell me:

What do you love to do?
What are you good at?
What can you be paid to do?
And what does the world need?

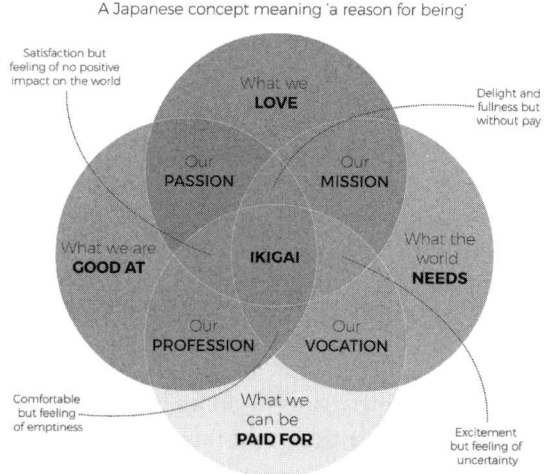

At the centre of these four questions, you will find your ikigai—something I detailed out in my first book, but in case you missed it or were too young to know or care—your ikigai is your life's true purpose. And if you find that *your* purpose leads you to a life and livelihood online, then all I ask is that you add a layer of humanity to your digital interactions. Whenever you find yourself about to go off at someone in the comments or feel deeply wounded by how they went off at you, picture a real human being on the other end and then proceed accordingly.

Fellow entrepreneur Anil Menghani very succinctly put down a few key takeaways from a talk of mine he attended and I think this is a pretty good checklist to start with:

1. Be effortless in whatever you do—by being your authentic self.
2. It takes time to find your ikigai—so have patience and passion.
3. Rather than collecting things—collect experiences.
4. Always focus on how to be a good listener.
5. Find the right people in your influence to keep you grounded.
6. Biggest mistake in personal branding—comparing yourself to others—so *stop* doing it!
7. Don't fake on social media—treat it like real life.
8. Have the right team members who believe in your vision/idea.
9. The only place where success comes before work is in the dictionary—so the first step is be prepared to do the work—hard work!
10. Don't take yourself so seriously.
11. Always be kinder than you think you have to.

And as far as that pound of flesh is concerned, remember this, the greatest relationship you will ever have is with yourself. Yes, the one taking that selfie in the mirror with main character energy.

You *are* the hero of your movie and I am a member of the supporting cast, just like I am the hero of my life and you are a supporting cast member. Now *you* decide the narrative. Is your main character a victim of social media or a vigilante? The kind of Robin Hood of good that gets off on spreading my favourite currency—positivity. I adopted the moniker Optimist Prime many years ago because I believe in happily ever after. For me, the story isn't over until there is a happy ending. So, the best advice I can possibly give you is this: approach your adventure as a comedy. Then, every tragic thing that happens, or every 'evil character' you encounter becomes a little less dangerous, to some degree a bumbling fool.

Whenever you find your digital avatar veering a little too far off course from your authentic self, do a little reboot, pause and ask yourself this question: What would the 'real' life me do? You're nicer than you think you are, just let the real you guide your virtual actions and practise copious amounts of kindness—it's the one thing that nobody can get enough or give enough of in any situation, real or virtual. And you can quote me on that!

It's Time to Spill Some Positivi-TEA!

So let's flip everything we know about social media on its head today. The three rules I encourage you to live by are:

- Never post anything you wouldn't say to someone's face.
- Remember that followers are people too.
- Spark joy (with your next post).

And from now on, let's stop worrying about how many likes we get or how many followers we have, let's start focusing on what we're putting out into the digital galaxy.

> *What if I told you the new currency of the internet is positivity? How much are you worth?*

What if it didn't matter anymore how many likes or followers you had, but the currency of karma was how much love you *gave* other people? What if your most valuable asset was positivity, of which—good news!—you had a never-ending supply! What if you could earn positivity points and spend them on doing good things, buying gifts, sharing experiences and whatever else ...

There are some incredible examples of how people have used social media to make a difference, spread joy, even elicit social change. That just goes to show that there *is* something bigger in our hands here ...

Can we go so far as to make the case that if social media existed in 1912 we could have spread the word and stopped the virus? That technology could have saved hundreds of millions of lives? If that is the case and we have it now, we should probably think about how we're using it before we post an obscenity or point out a fully clothed boob (true-story on my IG on the daily). Maybe we should treat it and its many inhabitants with a tad more respect and love.

I am happy to report that while there have been the occasional cases of trolling and anxiety-triggered anger in my orbit, for the most part I have seen love, compassion, friendship and, above all, authenticity. The empathy of shared suffering and even shared hope. It may be too soon to tell, but maybe, just maybe, the virus that so brutally infected our lungs will help disinfect our virtual programming ... which brings me to 2020's most popular hashtag: #spreadlovenotcorona

The Kindness of Strangers

Look at Johann Kuruvilla, a travel blogger from Kerala who joined WhatsApp groups to coordinate rescue efforts during the Kerala floods of 2019.

Lilly Singh, aka iiSuperwomanii, has this incredible #girllove campaign that encourages girls to build each other up instead of tearing each other down!

Look, I'm not saying everything is perfect and happy all the time. But what if we saw virtual reality as another form of reality? And you try to get your virtual avatar as close to your real identity and approach that world with as much empathy and kindness as you're able to?

As an experiment, I asked people on social media to answer these questions: If you had to describe your own 'virtual personality' vs your real-life personality, what would you say? Are they the same or different? And if so, in what way? Are you shy, snarky, impatient, positive, angry, easily amused, meme-obsessed, helpful, kind, cold, indifferent, emotional ... You get the idea.

Real-life me	Virtual me
My real-life personality is super friendly, enthu-cutlet, sometimes shy, insecure, short-tempered, nervous, funny, loving, ambitious and optimistic.	My virtual personality is bubbly, positive, emotional, sometimes oversensitive, often envious, but kind and empathetic.

How's that for some raw honesty? That felt good to say out loud. Thanks for listening. I am getting closer to merging my two avatars to be my one true complete self in both worlds, but it's a journey, it's a process.

I asked you answered ...[112]

Real-life me	Virtual me
Creative, love style, Over-emotional, super friendly, fun-loving, shy with new people, helpful and empathetic, nervous, good humour, loving, a fast learner, optimistic and aspiring …	Stylish, creative, confident, bold, carefree, often envious, but helpful and empathetic, sometimes misjudged as opportunist
Creative, emotional, friendly, fun, laugh at myself and others, boho chic, intelligent, empathetic and sometimes judgemental	Enthusiastic, sassy, throaty laugh from the heart, empathetic and good humour, creative
In reality I am a #nofilter kind of person—I laugh a lot and crack crazy jokes, hot tempered and impulsive—but only a few know me like that 😊	My virtual personality is very different because my handle is about my CEO life—so it shows my life experiences, travels and dreams more than anything.

📷 Your Turn, What's in Your Jar?

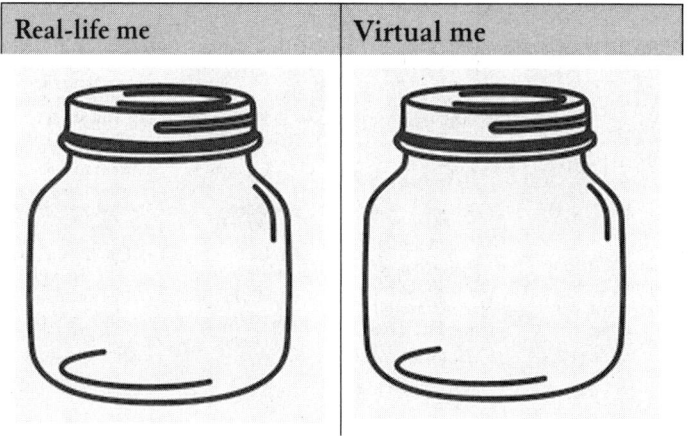

Real-life me	Virtual me

See, life may not be positive all the time, so how can we be expected to be? Fair. But sometimes it's up to us to generate that positivity, isn't it? To cancel out the sadness. Flood the grey with a world of colour. *Be* the rainbow!

Try it. Give someone a compliment and see what happens. They feel good, you feel good, everybody wins!

They say it takes twenty-one days to form a habit. Maxwell Maltz, a plastic surgeon in the 1950s, first introduced the twenty-one-day habit theory. He discovered that patients who had face surgery, for example, needed that many days to get used to seeing their new face![113]

How about we get used to seeing our new souls? Okay, that got heavy, LOL, but to set you on your path to virtual positivity (or help you course correct), I've set out an easy-to-follow schedule for sparking joy for twenty-one days. Please feel free to tag five friends to do this with you. I'll see you on the other side. And

I'll be reposting all your acts of sparking joy on my Instagram, so don't forget to tag me!

21-Day POSITIVITY CHALLENGE

DAY 1 — Pretend that EVERY person you see is a long lost friend and you LOVE them to pieces!

DAY 2 — Find your favourite inspiring quote and put it up in your home.

DAY 3 — Pay attention to what ENERGIZES you today and what DRAINS you.

DAY 4 — Do LESS of what drains you and MORE of what energizes you today.

DAY 5 — Ditch your 'to do' list and decide today how you're going 'to be'.

DAY 5 — Exercise for at least five minutes today.

DAY 7 — Listen to a song that makes you feel happy!

DAY 8 — Make eye contact with and smile at everyone you see.

DAY 9 — Choose only ONE thing on your 'to do' list to accomplish today.

DAY 10 — Treat someone you love to something AMAZING today.

DAY 11 — Write things that make you happy. Place them in a bag for when you're down.

DAY 12 — Choose one space in your home to declutter! Block out twenty minutes per day.

DAY 13 — Meditate. Imagine your mind as a snow globe. It needs to sit still to clear.

DAY 14 — You vs the Universe. What can you control? What can you surrender to a higher power?

DAY 15 — Start a vision board. When you see it, you will create it.

DAY 16 — Do something to step out of your comfort zone!

DAY 17 — Today, turn all your negative thoughts into positive ones.

DAY 18 — You want to be confident? What does that look like? Be specific. Fake it.

DAY 19 — Write a letter to future you and pop it up on your vision board. What have you accomplished?

DAY 20 — Start a mood journal and write it in every day.

DAY 21 — If you've completed these challenges, celebrate how far you've come.

Start today, start now. Take out your phone and put some love out into the universe.

If you want to use a filter, filter out the negativity! When you declutter your social media you will declutter your mind, when you surround yourself with endless optimism you will attract positivity. *If* we all make our mission the pursuit of happiness we won't have time for trolls or time to become one of them. If there is one thing I want you to take away from all this, it is this:

> *If you don't like what's on social media today, I challenge you to change what you put on it. It's time to take charge of your social media legacy.*

Someone once said, 'We are what we repeatedly do. Excellence is not an act, but a habit.' *Let's make positivity a habit.*

A Letter to your Eighteen-Year-Old Self

Perhaps your parents can bookmark it for you. Perhaps you're reading it now. Whatever the case may be, from me to you, here's the tea. Piping hot.

Dear eighteen-year-old you,

How's it going? I bet you weren't expecting this and I'm sorry. I'm pretty sure my generation had something significant to do with the world you live in today (or, rather, can't live in). I don't know where we screwed up exactly but, to be honest, I think we didn't expect to see any major life-altering repercussions in our lifetimes, so we probably didn't think enough about yours. But that's not the point of this letter. A few years ago, I wrote a letter to *my* eighteen-year-old-self where I remember telling myself that the most valuable currency of the world is 'time' and the young, who will inherit the earth, are wealthy in it. I have since grown 365 days (roughly what feels like a week in lockdown). And I think I was wrong.

In the podcast, *This American Life*, hosted by Ira Glass, I listened to an episode called 'Stuck' which he recorded inside his closet with the sound of hangers and shirts rustling in the background. We're all feeling, it right? This 'stuck-ness'? Heck, Ariana Grande and Justin Bieber made a song about it ('Stuck With U' already has 44 million views—very catchy)! Anyway, in this episode, he quotes Damon Linker, who writes for a website called The Week:

> [...] right now, with schools and jobs shut down, we've all become unmoored from the future, we're stuck in the present and it's unclear when we're going to move forward to graduation or a new job or whatever else we're building for ourselves and our lives in a normal time that we'd be looking forward to. And he tries to make the case that this is a big, big deal, 'human beings, live their lives in time', he [Damon] writes. Our sense of ourselves is probably who we are trying to become. Quote, 'a life without forward momentum is to a considerable extent, a life without purpose, or at least the kind of purpose that lifts our spirits and livens our steps. Without the momentum and purpose we flounder. A present without a future is a life that feels less worth living because it's a life haunted by a shadow of futility.'[114]

But I'm here to tell you that I don't think that's true. Sure, it might feel that way if you've been told all your life that your purpose and measure of success will be all the degrees you collect, or promotions you secure, the fancy grown-up toys you'll flex on Instagram and the virtual popularity contests you'll win ... 'one day' (someday, but never today).

But what if that's not what it's about at all?

I have spent my life saying, and truly believing, that I feel like we did it all wrong. You know, life. We got caught up in the wrong things. We weren't put on this planet for an eighty- to a hundred-odd years to join some collective race (like rats or otherwise). We weren't given the power to contemplate our own existence to all blindly follow some 'proven path' to success that's measured largely by wealth and fame. We're here because (as cheesy as it sounds, and I tattooed it on my ribs, I'm *that* sure):

The greatest thing you'll ever learn is just to love, and be loved in return.

The film *Moulin Rouge* (2001) taught me that (for you that's an oldie but it's a goldy, I promise).

And it isn't always romantic love; it could be loving the planet, your adventures, your life, your friends, yourself. Let me ask you, how much time have you spent loving sitting at a desk for eight hours a day? Waiting for a 'time' when you can really enjoy your life? That weekend, that vacation, when you retire ...

Maybe you have a chance to fix this. Maybe, this collective pause button that has been pressed by some force in the universe is to give you *the time* to reassess what you want to do with yours. What if I was wrong about all the times I was telling myself I had to do things, to be someone, not realizing I already was? Someone, that is.

I have always had trouble being in the moment, I struggle with the 'now', I'm always one WhatsApp conversation away from being distracted and I have truly always believed that happiness is nothing more than having something to look forward to. That means I have never really gotten there; I've just lived in the intoxicating anticipation of it ...

But if all we have is right now, and today something has actually erased the concept of 'a future' we recognize for us maybe you, my dear eighteen-year-old, are inheriting an earth you can actually be present in. Maybe now, with no predetermined concept of success or proven path you're expected to follow, you have the opportunity to build a new world. A new way of being. Maybe you're reading this sentence right now being absolutely present, while I sit here typing in the anticipation that you will ...

And as Emily Dickinson so wisely said, 'Forever is composed of Nows'—outside the scope of memory, there is only here and now ... time is merely a series of 'nows'.

I am so excited for you. All I had was time, you have all of *now*.

Epilogue

Fame & Accomplishment—The Difference Is Key

> *No one can stop you from shinning if you are standing in your own light.*
> —Matshona Dhliwayo

Occasionally, people ask me what it feels like to be famous. Truth be told, I don't think of myself as 'famous' but I understand the question. I guess I've accomplished some stuff that has resulted in a certain level of positive infamy for sure (and don't get me wrong, I low-key love it) but I'm not *famous* famous and I kinda like it that way and I'll tell you why. When fame fades (and it always does), people might point at you as you go by and say, 'Oh, look, there goes so-and-so, they used to be someone famous.' But they won't say that about someone who has *accomplished* something. Nobody can take away your accomplishments. They'll always have to say 'look there goes so-and-so, this is what she accomplished!'

Fame is fleeting but nobody can take away your accomplishments, and when you're less worried about losing something you're a lot nicer about letting other people have it too. So my advice to you, hand on heart, is spend a little more time on the internet trying to accomplish something and worry less about trying to be famous (or ripping apart someone who already is) and you'll find that you live in a kinder world. To quote an epic quote you've probably heard me say so many times because it's the truest thing I've ever heard:

You don't need to unscrew anybody else's light bulb to shine.

Acknowledgements

This book would not have been possible without the support and encouragement of my friends and family, and my fabulous agent Anuj, and, of course, my publishers at HarperCollins India who believed I had not one but two books in me right from the start.

It would be remiss of me not to thank social media as a medium for giving me my whole extraordinary life, and that means everyone on it who has ever been my witness via a double tap, a share, a comment or a like. Thank you for not letting my life go unnoticed, thank you for not letting my life go unwitnessed. (This will all make more sense if you read my first book btw 😊 #iykyk).

Notes, Appendix and Sources

The detailed notes, appendix and sources pertaining to this book are available on the HarperCollins *Publishers* India website. Scan this QR code to access the same.

Book Cover Credits

Photographer: Rohan Shrestha
Make-up by: Elton J. Fernandez
Outfit by: Rudraksh Dwivedi
Styled by: Rishika Devnani
Shades by: The Half Done
Photographer assistant: Homyar Patel
Make-up assistant: Shristi Mishra
Styling assistant: Vanshika Makkar

Team MissMalini
Manager: Yeansha Lodha
Executive assistant: Neelabh Saxena
Social media executive: Dhruv Sodha
Social media executive: Siddhi Jain

About the Author

Malini Agarwal is among the first globally recognized Indian influencers, as well as the founder and creative director of MissMalini Entertainment and co-founder of Good Creator Co. She is also the founder of a community for women called Girl Tribe by MissMalini, which was created to serve as a safe place for women to talk, share, support, empower, network and inspire each other to live their best lives.

MissMalini Entertainment's goal has always been to become a media brand that connects influencers and consumers. Good Creator Co.—India's largest and most comprehensive creator ecosystem—was founded following an acquisition by the Good Glamm Group and the desire to create the ultimate universe for content creators.

Her first book, the bestselling *To the Moon: How I Blogged My Way to Bollywood*, was published by HarperCollins India in 2018.

HarperCollins *Publishers* India

At HarperCollins India, we believe in telling the best stories and finding the widest readership for our books in every format possible. We started publishing in 1992; a great deal has changed since then, but what has remained constant is the passion with which our authors write their books, the love with which readers receive them, and the sheer joy and excitement that we as publishers feel in being a part of the publishing process.

Over the years, we've had the pleasure of publishing some of the finest writing from the subcontinent and around the world, including several award-winning titles and some of the biggest bestsellers in India's publishing history. But nothing has meant more to us than the fact that millions of people have read the books we published, and that somewhere, a book of ours might have made a difference.

As we look to the future, we go back to that one word— a word which has been a driving force for us all these years.

Read.

Harper Collins

HARPER PERENNIAL

HARPER BUSINESS

HARPER BLACK

हार्पर हिन्दी

HarperCollins *Children'sBooks*

HARPER DESIGN

HARPER VANTAGE

Harper Sport